POND LIFE

A GUIDE TO COMMON PLANTS AND ANIMALS OF NORTH AMERICAN PONDS AND LAKES

by
GEORGE K. REID, Ph.D.

Under the editorship of
HERBERT S. ZIM
and
GEORGE S. FICHTER

Illustrated by
SALLY D. KAICHER
and
TOM DOLAN

GOLDEN PRESS • NEW YORK
Western Publishing Company, Inc.
Racine, Wisconsin

FOREWORD

A pond or a lake offers an opportunity for exciting dis-
coveries. There one can become acquainted with many
kinds of plants and animals and learn how they live together in a community. This book describes and illus-
trates some of the most common of the thousands of species of plants and animals found in or near these waters.
Some are more at home in clear, cool lakes than in shallow, warm ponds. Others are found in streams as well as
in still waters or may grow in the nearby wetlands.

Many persons have contributed to this book. The art-
ists, Mrs. Sally Kaicher and Mr. Tom Dolan, have ren-
dered accurate illustrations. Professors Murray F. Buell,
of Rutgers University, and Robert W. Pennak, of the
University of Colorado, provided photographs from
which illustrations were made. The University of South
Florida permitted liberal use of library facilities. Thanks
are due also to colleagues, experts, and organizations
for their invaluable help in providing specimens or in
checking the text for accuracy and usefulness.   G.K.R.

CONTENTS

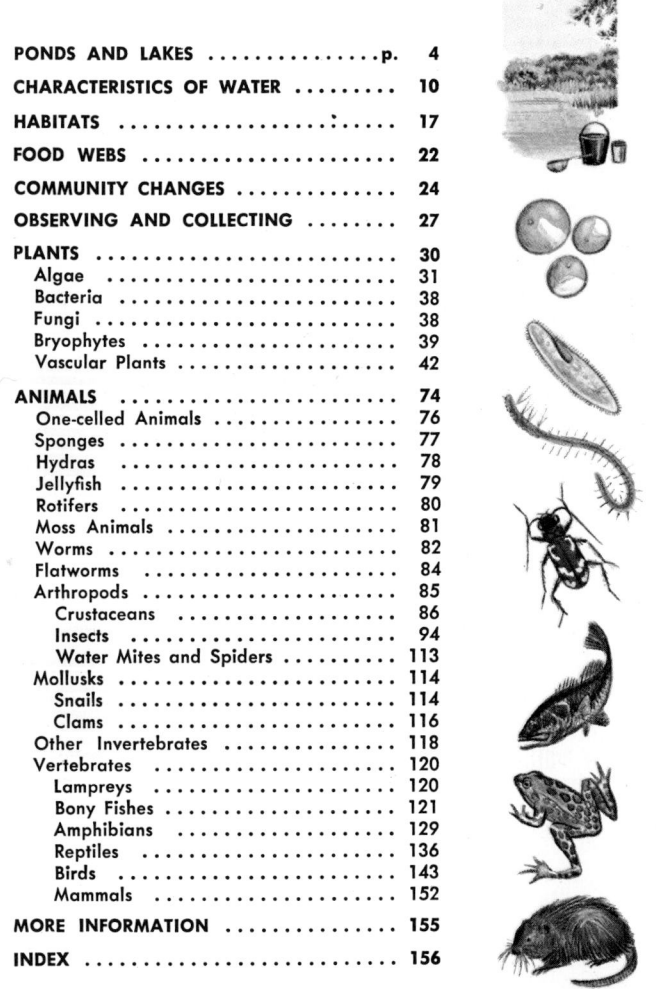

PONDS AND LAKES ....p. 4

CHARACTERISTICS OF WATER 10

HABITATS 17

FOOD WEBS 22

COMMUNITY CHANGES 24

OBSERVING AND COLLECTING 27

PLANTS 30
  Algae 31
  Bacteria 38
  Fungi 38
  Bryophytes 39
  Vascular Plants 42

ANIMALS 74
  One-celled Animals 76
  Sponges 77
  Hydras 78
  Jellyfish 79
  Rotifers 80
  Moss Animals 81
  Worms 82
  Flatworms 84
  Arthropods 85
    Crustaceans 86
    Insects 94
    Water Mites and Spiders 113
  Mollusks 114
    Snails 114
    Clams 116
  Other Invertebrates 118
  Vertebrates 120
    Lampreys 120
    Bony Fishes 121
    Amphibians 129
    Reptiles 136
    Birds 143
    Mammals 152

MORE INFORMATION 155

INDEX 156

Spring

Summer

PONDS AND LAKES

In spring and summer, activity is ceaseless in a pond or small lake. Water striders skate over the surface. Dragonfly nymphs, which will soon change into swift, darting adults, climb the stems of cattails. Close to shore a crayfish grabs and eats a worm—and moments later a bass devours the crayfish. A turtle plops off a log and begins to browse on plants. Countless small shrimplike copepods strain their microscopic plant food from the water and then become food for small fishes that, in turn, are eaten by large fishes or by wading birds. As the water cools in autumn, animals become less active. In winter, the pond or lake is rather quiet, and in the North, only a few animals still stir under the ice.

Fall   Winter

To understand the teeming life in a pond, one must know what conditions are necessary to support it. This study of inland waters—ponds, lakes, and streams—is called limnology. It is a division of the broader science of ecology, which deals with the ways plants and animals live together in particular environments. Limnology is concerned with all the interrelated factors that influence the inland-water environment. Thus it treats not only biology but also chemistry, geography, weather, climate, and other similar factors or conditions. Only a few of the many thousands of plants and animals that live in or near ponds, lakes, and streams are described and illustrated in this book. As your interest in "pond probing" grows you can consult the books listed on page 155 for more detailed information.

A POND is commonly described by limnologists as a quiet body of water so shallow that rooted plants grow completely across it. Its water temperature is fairly uniform from top to bottom and tends to change with the air temperature. There is little wave action, and the bottom is usually covered with mud. Typically, plants grow all along the shore. The amount of dissolved oxygen may vary greatly in a 24-hour period.

A lake is usually larger than a pond. The water is too deep for plants to grow except around the shore. The temperature of the water is relatively stable from day to day, but in northern lakes, temperature "layering" oc-

curs in summer (p. 15). The amount of dissolved oxygen during a 24-hour period remains about the same. Because of the broad expanse of water exposed to the wind, shores on the down-wind side are commonly wave-washed, barren strands of sand or rocks.

What people know as a pond or a lake locally, however, differs from one region to another. In some places, for example, the pond illustrated on p. 6 would be called a marsh. Many of the broad lakes in Florida are shallow, and though they lack plants in the middle, their water temperature and amount of dissolved oxygen follow the pattern of ponds.

SEVERAL DIFFERENT KINDS of bodies of water are called ponds. The basins of some ponds are potholes in glacial debris and are filled by seepage and runoff water from the surrounding land. Others are cutoffs from old stream channels. Some are temporary, others permanent. Despite their differences in origin and age, all are much alike in size, depth, and similar features. A few of the more common and distinctive kinds of ponds are shown here.

CYPRESS PONDS are common in the central and lower Mississippi Basin and along the coastal plain of the southeastern U.S. Their water is often brownish, and many are dry during parts of the year. Along the shore, willows and bay trees are mixed with cypresses, which often grow out into the water.   Above.

BOG PONDS are found in moist temperate regions over most of N.A. Their water is usually highly acid and is often muddy. Cedars dominate the high ground, and alders grow profusely on the shore. Thick beds of sphagnum extend outward from shore. Floating-leaf plants may cover the surface.   Below.

MEADOW-STREAM PONDS develop where a stream widens and the speed of its current drops sharply. Pondweeds, stoneworts, cattails, and others with emergent leaves grow in the shallows. Water lilies, water shield, and others send floating leaves to the surface.   Above.

MOUNTAIN PONDS are often formed by glaciers. In some, the bottom is pure rock; in others, deep, soft mud. Many are ice-free only briefly and dry up in summer. Sedges grow along margins. Despite the short summer season, many kinds of animals live in these icy waters.

FARM PONDS are built as a part of good farming practices. They also provide fishing and boating. A farm pond should be at least 3 feet deep at the shoreline to prevent plant growth and have a spillway to control water level. It should fill from seepage, not from a stream that will soon fill the basin with silt.

9

Water will dissolve more substances than will any other liquid, and for this reason it is called "the universal solvent." Oxygen, carbon dioxide, and nitrogen are absorbed from the atmosphere. Oxygen is also contributed as a by-product of photosynthesis (p. 30), and carbon dioxide is released by both plants and animals in respiration (p. 12). Phosphates, chlorides, and similar mineral salts are dissolved in run-off and seepage water.

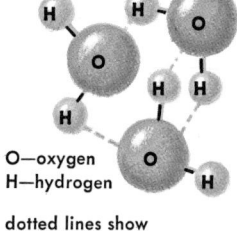

O—oxygen
H—hydrogen

dotted lines show
hydrogen bonds in
water molecules

WATER MOLECULES are strongly attracted to one another through their two hydrogen atoms. At the surface this attraction produces a tight film over the water. A number of organisms live both on the upper and on the lower sides of this surface film (p. 17).

DENSITY OF WATER is greatest at 4°C (39.2°F). It becomes less as water warms and, more important, as it cools to freezing at 0°C. Then it changes to ice which floats as its density is only 0.917. Ice is also a poor conductor and thus reduces heat loss from below. Only very shallow ponds ever freeze solid.

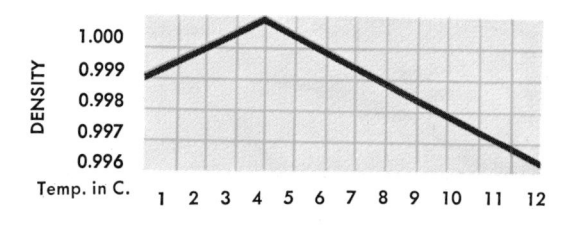

DENSITY
1.000
0.999
0.998
0.997
0.996
Temp. in C.   1 2 3 4 5 6 7 8 9 10 11 12

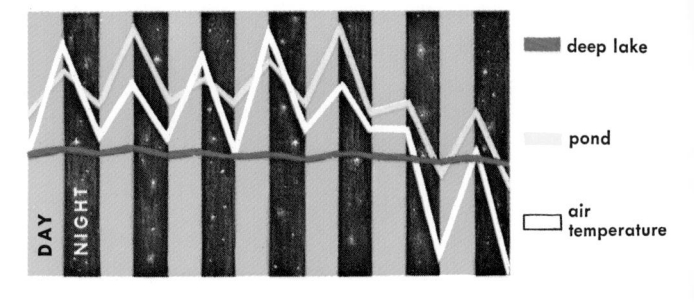

deep lake

pond

air
temperature

HEAT-HOLDING CAPACITY of water is great. It absorbs and releases heat much more slowly than does air. For this reason plants and animals of most ponds and lakes are not usually subjected to suddenly varied temperatures. Though the air temperature may change rapidly and greatly, the water temperature of a deep lake changes slowly. In a shallow pond or lake, the water temperature varies with the air temperature, as above.

TRANSPARENCY OF WATER permits enough light to penetrate for plants to carry on photosynthesis. The depth to which light can penetrate decreases as water becomes more turbid or contains more suspended materials. Few plants grow in muddy ponds because the silt absorbs light.

	Clear Lake			Turbid Lake
	40%	3 ft.	20%	
	25%	9 ft.	5%	
	20%	15 ft.	0	

LIGHT PENETRATION

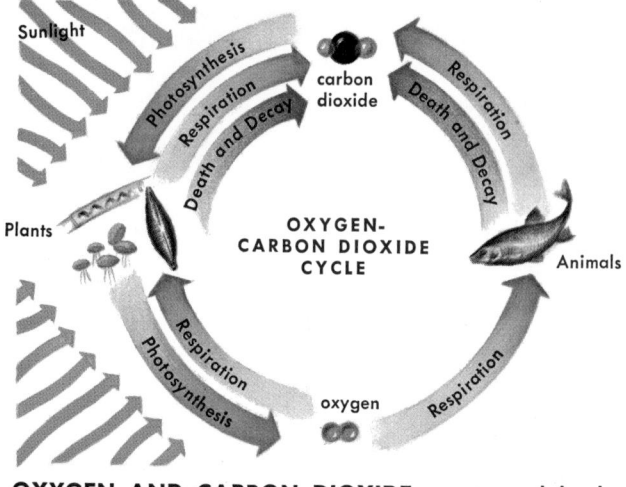

Sunlight

Photosynthesis Respiration Death and Decay

carbon dioxide

Respiration Death and Decay

OXYGEN-CARBON DIOXIDE CYCLE

Plants

Animals

Respiration Photosynthesis

oxygen

Respiration

OXYGEN AND CARBON DIOXIDE are passed back and forth between plants and animals and their environment. The proportion of these gases in the atmosphere is generally constant: oxygen, 21 percent; carbon dioxide, .03 percent. In pond, lake, and stream waters they usually vary greatly, even from night to day.

Oxygen, which is necessary for the survival of nearly all plants and animals, is quite soluble in water, but the amount dissolved in fresh water is much lower than in the atmosphere. Oxygen from the air is absorbed slowly, but the process is speeded when wind and waves disturb the water surface. Also, the cooler the water, the more dissolved oxygen it will hold.

During the day, when sunlight penetrates the water, plants give off oxygen as a by-product of photosynthesis more rapidly than it is used in respiration by plants and animals. A reserve of oxygen builds up. In darkness, when photosynthesis stops, both plants and animals use

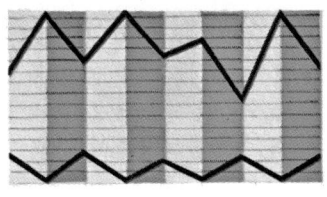

Oxygen level in a pond builds up by day, drops at night. Carbon dioxide follows reverse cycle.

Oxygen

Carbon Dioxide

■ day ■ night

this oxygen. For this reason the oxygen content in ponds and shallow lakes varies greatly in a 24-hour period.

Carbon dioxide, more soluble in water than oxygen, comes both from the decay of organic material and from respiration of plants and animals. Some is also contributed by ground water and from the atmosphere, either directly or with rain. Near the bottom of deep lakes the amount of dissolved carbon dioxide may be quite high. Few plants and animals can survive in this region. Carbon dioxide is used by plants in photosynthesis. It is the source of the carbon found in fats, proteins, and carbohydrates, the basic food substances of animals.

Carbon dioxide is important also in determining the water's pH—its degree of acidity or alkalinity. It combines with water to form weak carbonic acid, which in turn reacts with limestone or dissolved lime, if present, to form carbonates and bicarbonates. These compounds are indirect sources of carbon and serve also as "buffers" that regulate pH. The pH of water often determines what animals and plants live there (below). For example, mollusks with limy shells cannot live in acid waters.

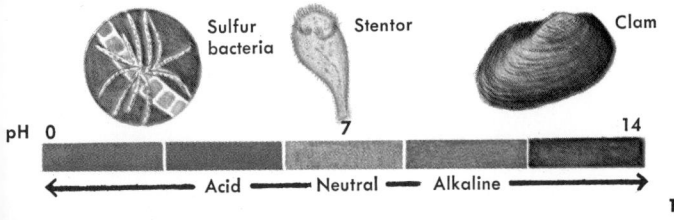

Sulfur bacteria Stentor Clam

pH 0 7 14

← Acid — Neutral — Alkaline →

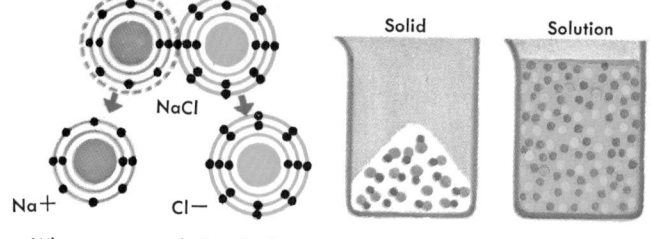

When common salt (NaCl) dissolves, it separates into ions (Na+ and Cl−) that diffuse throughout the solution.

DISSOLVED MINERALS in pond, lake, and stream waters include phosphates, nitrates, chlorides, sulfates, carbonates, and others. These "minerals" originated in chemical combination with such elements as potassium, magnesium, calcium, sodium, and iron. In solution these compounds are separated into their component ions. (For example, calcium carbonate, $CaCO_3$ becomes Ca^{++} and CO_3^{--}.) The minerals are absorbed by plants as ions rather than as salts. All plants and animals require small amounts of these minerals in building cell protoplasm and body tissues. Floating plants take their minerals directly from the water; rooted aquatic plants, from the pond bottom. Animals get minerals from their plant and animal foods. Minerals are released also from plants and animals that die and decay in the pond or lake. Thus the minerals are kept in cycle.

Floating mat of green algae (1) gets minerals from water, the rooted plant (2) from the pond bottom, and the turtle (3) from its plant food.

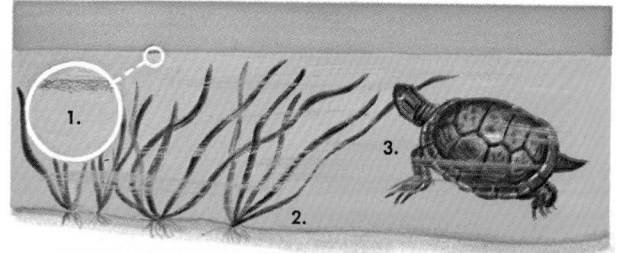

TEMPERATURE LAYERING occurs in deep lakes of temperate zones. In summer, the surface water absorbs the sun's heat and warms faster than the water below. The warmed water is less dense than the cold water, so it floats on the cool lower layers. By midsummer there are three distinct layers.

Not enough light penetrates the middle and lower layers to permit photosynthesis, and a mixing or circulation of water between the upper and lower levels is prevented by the thermocline, a layer of sudden temperature drop that acts as a barrier to vertical movements. Also, decomposition of organic debris in the lower layer increases the amount of carbon dioxide and reduces oxygen there. In these deep bodies of water nearly all of the fishes and other animals live above the thermocline, where food and oxygen are plentiful.

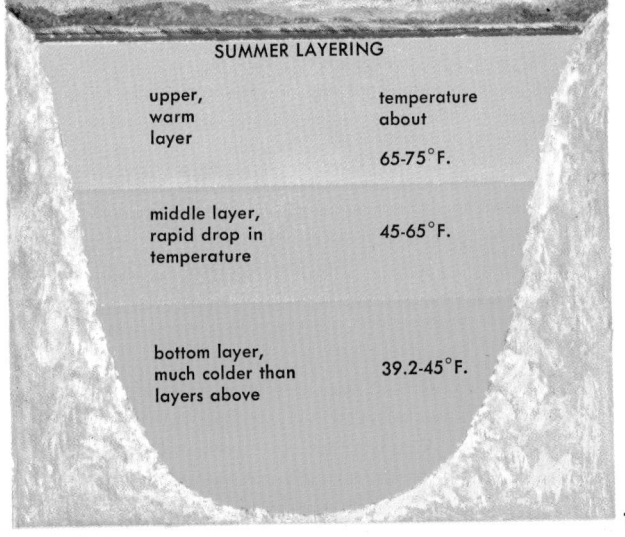

SUMMER LAYERING

upper, warm layer	temperature about 65-75°F.
middle layer, rapid drop in temperature	45-65°F.
bottom layer, much colder than layers above	39.2-45°F.

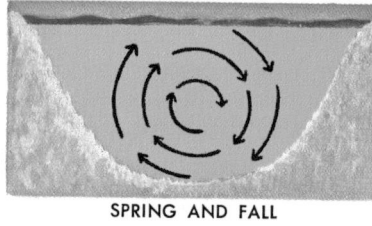

During spring and fall overturns, the temperature of the water is equalized throughout the lake. Fishes and other animals are active and widely distributed.

SPRING AND FALL

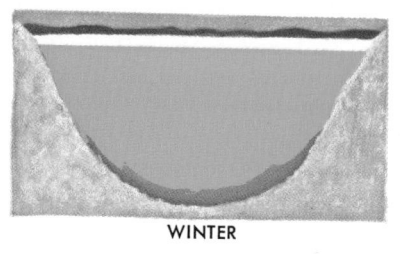

Activity is greatly reduced in winter, under the ice. Many animals hibernate in the mud or debris at the bottom. Some fishes continue to feed but less actively.

WINTER

The upper layer of water cools in autumn until it approaches the temperature of the water in the middle and lower layers. Aided by winds, the surface water sinks, causing circulation from top to bottom. This is called "fall overturn." In winter, the cold surface water continues to sink until, near the freezing point, its density begins to decrease. The near-freezing water (below 39.2°F.) eventually turns to ice at the surface.

The cover of ice prevents the wind from circulating the water, and "winter stagnation" occurs. Thick ice or snow also screens out the light and may stop photosynthesis. Plants and animals may die due to a lack of oxygen; this is called "winterkill." When the ice melts in spring and the surface water warms above 39.2°F., it becomes more dense. Aided by winds, another circulation and mixing, called "spring overturn," occurs until the water temperature is again relatively uniform.

HABITATS
IN PONDS AND LAKES

Habitats are places in which rather distinctive groups of plants and animals are found. In lakes and large ponds, the four easily recognized habitats are the surface film, open water, bottom, and shore.

THE SURFACE FILM is the habitat of air-breathing, floating animals and of those animals with special devices that permit them to walk on the surface without breaking through. Some kinds of beetles, water bugs, and free-floating plants are adapted to life only on the upper side of the film. The larvae of some beetles and flies spend much time hanging on the underside of the film. Surface-dwelling animals feed on the floating plants, prey on one another, or eat insects or other animals that drown and then float on the surface.

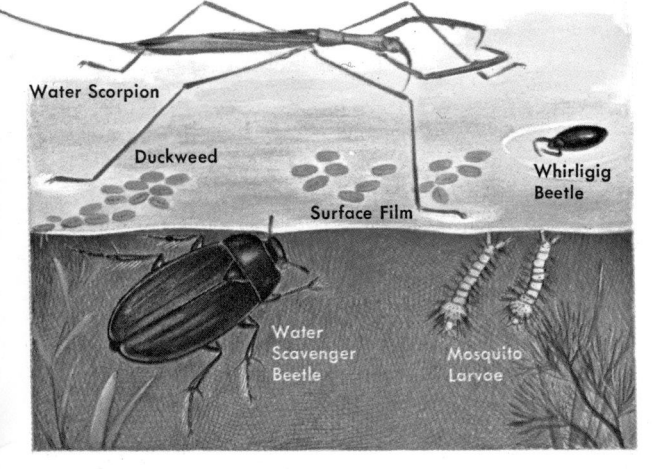

Water Scorpion

Duckweed

Surface Film

Whirligig Beetle

Water Scavenger Beetle

Mosquito Larvae

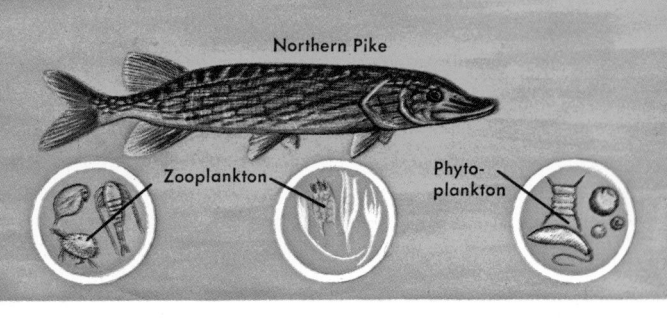

Northern Pike

Zooplankton

Phyto-plankton

OPEN-WATER life consists of large, free-swimming animals, such as the fishes, and of small microscopic plants and animals that drift suspended in the water. The drifters, called plankton, vastly outnumber all the larger pond inhabitants. Small suspended plants, or phytoplankton, are mostly algae, the basic food in ponds and lakes. At times, some phytoplankton species multiply in great numbers, forming a "bloom" that clouds the water. The zooplankton consists of small suspended animals—numerous tiny crustaceans, rotifers, some insect larvae, and other invertebrates. The kinds and numbers of plankton organisms vary seasonally but are usually most abundant in spring.

Turtles, birds, and large fishes frequent the open-water area. Small fishes usually remain among plants near shore. At night, some kinds of insect larvae and crustaceans migrate from the bottom toward the surface, then return to deeper water as daylight comes.

The open-water area ends where plants become rooted. Ponds and shallow lakes with emergent plants extending from shore to shore lack an open-water area. Deep open water of large lakes supports little or no life.

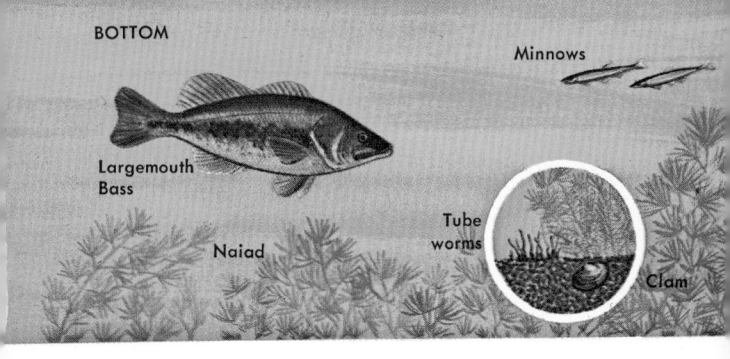

BOTTOM

Minnows

Largemouth
Bass

Naiad

Tube
worms

Clam

THE BOTTOM of ponds and lakes offers a variety of living conditions from the shore outward to the deepest regions. A sandy bottom in the shallows (p. 20) may be inhabited by sponges, snails, earthworms, and insects. If the water is quiet, the bottom is usually covered with mud or silt and contains much organic debris. Crayfish and the nymphs of mayflies, dragonflies, and damselflies are some of the many kinds of animals that burrow into the bottom muds. Others live among the plants, where food is usually plentiful and where they find protection from predators.

Living conditions on the bottom in deep open water are quite different. If the lake is very deep or the water turbid, light does not penetrate to the bottom and plants cannot grow. Animals can find little shelter, the amount of dissolved oxygen is low, and the carbon-dioxide concentration is high. Among the few larger animals that can live in the deep bottom zone are some of the earthworms, small clams, and fly larvae ("bloodworms" and "phantoms"). Bacteria of decay are commonly abundant in the deep region. They are important in returning chemicals to the cycle of life.

Water Lily

SUBMERSED

FLOATING

Pondweed   Catfish

Water Celery

Clam

Water Milfoil

THE LITTORAL HABITAT extends from the water's edge outward as far as rooted plants grow. In most ponds and in many shallow lakes, this area may stretch from shore to shore. In many lakes there are typically three distinct concentric borders of flowering plants, except where the shore is so rocky or swept by waves that plants cannot grow.

Closest to shore is the *emergent plant zone*. It is dominated by plants that are rooted to the bottom and have stems and leaves above the surface. Grasses, sedges, and rushes are plants typical of the emergent zone in ponds and lakes the world over. Many kinds of frogs, birds, and mammals find food and shelter here. A variety of algae, protozoans, worms, insects, snails, and small fishes live among underwater plant stems.

Broad, flat-leaved water lilies and such floating plants as water ferns and duckweeds characterize the *floating-leaf plant zone*. Because the masses of floating leaves shade out the light, bottom plants may be scarce. Some snails, bugs, and mayflies lay their eggs on the underside of leaves. Many kinds of algae live in this zone,

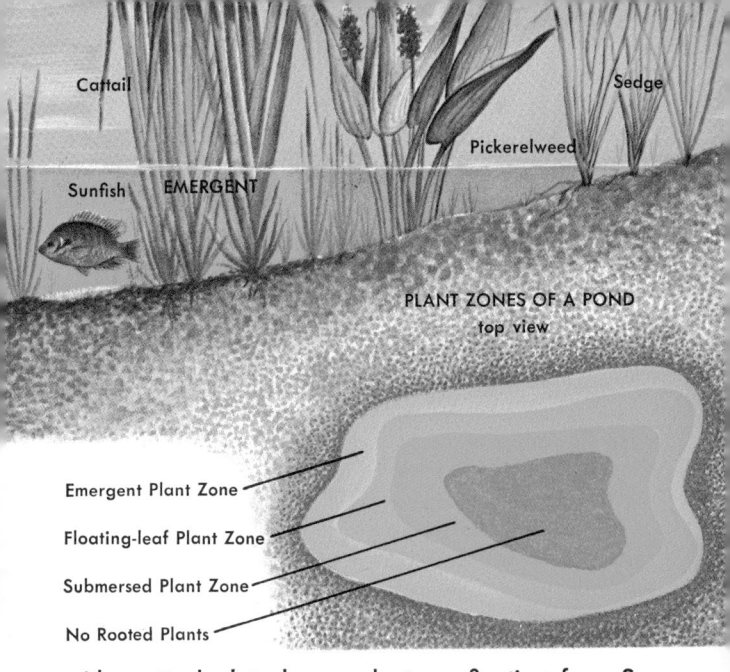

Cattail

Sedge

Pickerelweed

Sunfish   EMERGENT

PLANT ZONES OF A POND
top view

Emergent Plant Zone

Floating-leaf Plant Zone

Submersed Plant Zone

No Rooted Plants

either attached to larger plants or floating free. Sunfishes and others breed and nest here.

The innermost band of vegetation forms the *submersed
plant zone*. Pondweeds, hornworts, and waterweeds are
typical of this zone. All have leaves that are either long
and sinuous or bushy and very branched, characteristic
adaptations of those few flowering plants that grow
completely submerged. The flowers are pollinated above
the surface; the seeds germinate and the young plants
develop only under the water.

The littoral zone, dominated by higher plants is the
richest in the pond community. Here are the greatest
number of species, both plant and animal. The littoral
zone is easiest for the observer to visit and to study.

FOOD WEBS

Except for sunlight, the source of energy needed by green plants for photosynthesis, a pond or a lake either contains or produces everything necessary for the survival of the plants and animals that live in or near it. Ponds, because they are usually small, are especially good places in which to learn the relationships of plants and animals to their environment and to one another. The most common linkage is through production or consumption of food.

All green plants, from floating microscopic plants to such flowering plants as pond lilies, manufacture food. Plants become food for plant-eating (herbivorous) animals, such as mayfly nymphs, small crustaceans, and some kinds of beetles. These animals are in turn preyed upon by small flesh-eating (carnivorous) animals including fishes, dragonfly nymphs, and beetle larvae. Larger fishes eat the smaller fishes, crustaceans, and insects. If not eaten, every plant and animal eventually dies and decomposes. Its protoplasm is reduced to the basic materials that green plants need for growth. In this way the cycle of foods is continuous.

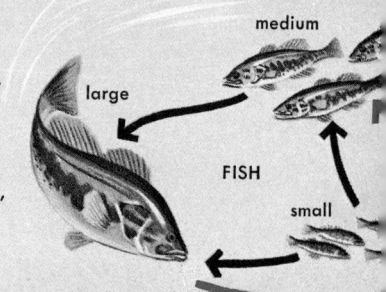

In ponds, food webs (chains or pyramids) may be complex, with many direct and indirect food sources supplying consumers. All, however, can be traced ultimately to green plants, the primary food producers, which derive energy from the sun. This diagram shows a few food relationships. The black arrows show the most direct, most important paths; the red, those of lesser importance.

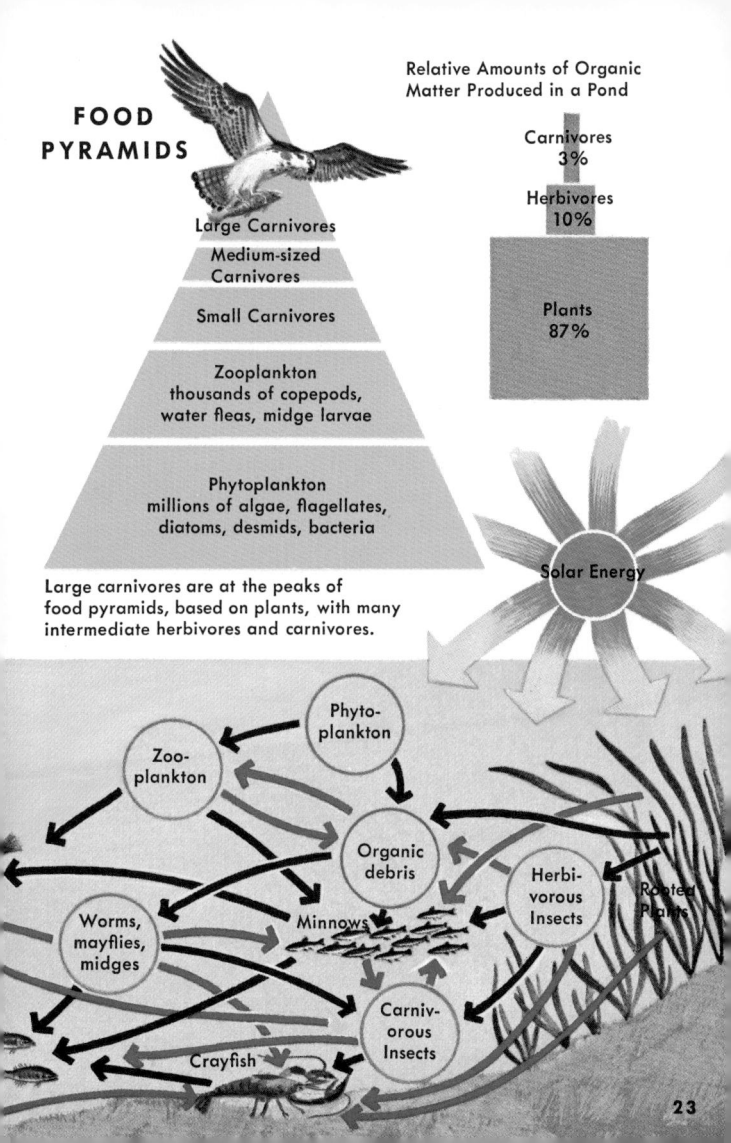

FOOD PYRAMIDS

Relative Amounts of Organic Matter Produced in a Pond

Carnivores 3%

Herbivores 10%

Plants 87%

Large Carnivores

Medium-sized Carnivores

Small Carnivores

Zooplankton
thousands of copepods, water fleas, midge larvae

Phytoplankton
millions of algae, flagellates, diatoms, desmids, bacteria

Large carnivores are at the peaks of food pyramids, based on plants, with many intermediate herbivores and carnivores.

Solar Energy

Phyto-plankton

Zoo-plankton

Organic debris

Herbi-vorous Insects

Rooted Plants

Worms, mayflies, midges

Minnows

Carnivorous Insects

Crayfish

23

COMMUNITY CHANGES IN PONDS AND LAKES

The number and kinds of plants and animals making up a pond or lake community changes continuously. These orderly and progressive changes are called "succession." Some of the changes are rapid, others come slowly. Often it takes hundreds of years for the succession of life in a pond to be completed. Various stages of maturation can often be seen in the different ponds in one region. In its young stage, organic matter from pioneer plants and animals and from debris has just begun to accumulate in the pond (1). In time, seeds of a few emergent plants are carried to the pond by the wind, water, or pond-visiting animals, and plants begin to line the shore (2). Then small fishes, snails, mussels, caddisflies, mayflies, and dragonflies find sufficient food to live in the pond. Some arrive as eggs carried on the feet of

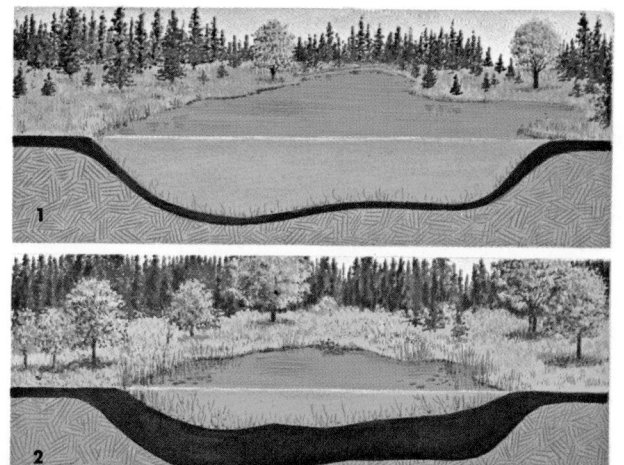

birds or other pond visitors. Adult insects may fly from pond to pond; frogs, turtles, mice, and other large animals travel over land.

Eventually pondweeds become abundant on the bottom, and the emergent shore plants grow farther out into the pond. All contribute more and more organic matter to the bottom as they die and decay. And, as the plant population changes in character, the kinds of fishes, insects, and other animals also change.

Finally emergent vegetation extends all the way across the pond, which now may be called a marsh (3). (Marshes may also originate in other ways.) Bullheads, salamanders, frogs, and turtles are the dominant large animals; worms live in the thick bottom mud, and many aquatic insects are found in the shallow, weedy waters. Land plants close in around the shore, growing in the rich humus. The filling continues until what was once a pond becomes either a grassy prairie or a forest (4). This is the stabilized or climax stage.

Changes in the community also occur from day to night and from one season to the next. Many animals stay in burrows or hide in the dense plant growth by day. At night they emerge and move about in search of food. Some planktonic crustaceans float to the surface at night, then return to the depths during the day. After a quiet winter, with the pond often beneath ice, life flourishes again with spring warming. Plants bloom, immature insects molt and take off in swarming flights of adults, fishes spawn, and frogs and turtles emerge from hibernation. Activity continues throughout the summer, then subsides in autumn as winter approaches and the temperature of the water drops.

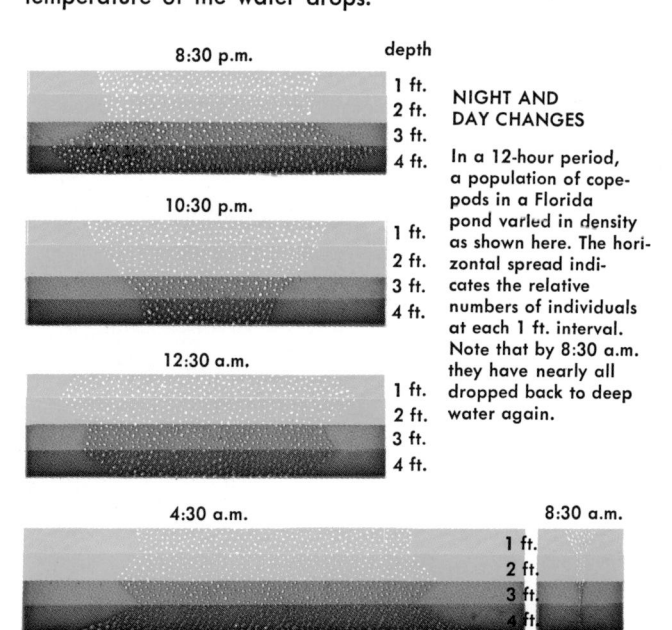

8:30 p.m.

depth
1 ft.
2 ft.
3 ft.
4 ft.

10:30 p.m.

1 ft.
2 ft.
3 ft.
4 ft.

12:30 a.m.

1 ft.
2 ft.
3 ft.
4 ft.

4:30 a.m.

8:30 a.m.

1 ft.
2 ft.
3 ft.
4 ft.

NIGHT AND DAY CHANGES

In a 12-hour period, a population of copepods in a Florida pond varied in density as shown here. The horizontal spread indicates the relative numbers of individuals at each 1 ft. interval. Note that by 8:30 a.m. they have nearly all dropped back to deep water again.

OBSERVING AND COLLECTING

Many of the plants and animals of ponds and lakes can be observed and identified in their natural surroundings. Often, however, it is necessary to collect them for closer inspection, or small plants and animals may be kept in aquariums to learn more about their habits. It is interesting to note the adaptations of plants and animals to various habitats (p. 17) and to observe the variations in types found in different kinds of ponds.

Large plants and animals do not require special or expensive collecting equipment. Common household utensils or easily constructed items can be used. Special equipment can be bought from biological supply firms.

Abundance of life along and in ponds rewards both observer and collector.

NETS and other straining devices are essential for collecting. To catch flying insects, use a cone-shaped net of fine-meshed cloth on a round frame and attached to a long handle. A bag-shaped net on a very stout frame with a strong handle is used in the water, or a piece of window screen mounted between two sticks can be used for collecting among plants or litter. Catch fishes and larger animals in a minnow seine.

Plankton nets are made of very fine-meshed cloth. At least 180 meshes to the inch are needed for phytoplankton. A fairly satisfactory net for larger plankton animals can be made by attaching the upper part of a lady's stocking to a hoop of proper size. Then cut off the foot and tie the cut end around the neck of a jar. The net can be drawn through the water (p. 27), or water dipped from the pond and poured through it.

WHITE ENAMEL PANS are useful for sorting through debris caught in the hand net. A little of the debris is put into a pan half filled with water. The live animals are soon seen moving about over the white bottom. Forceps are the most practical instruments for transferring specimens.

A WATERSCOPE, OR UNDER-WATER VIEWER, can be made by sealing a piece of glass in a bottomless bucket or water-proofed box. Commercial water-scopes are available also.

A PLANT HOOK (grapple) attached to a line is useful for pulling in plants from deep water for examination.

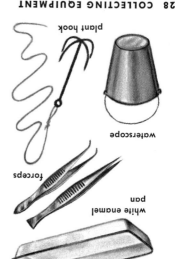

plant hook

waterscope

forceps

white enamel pan

net for flying insects

aquatic net

sieve

KILLING JARS for insects can be made of a wad of cotton soaked with cleaning fluid (carbon tetrachloride) placed in the bottom of a screw-cap jar. Other types of killing jars can be bought from biological supply houses.

VIALS AND JARS containing a preservative are important to have on a collecting trip. Jars with screw caps are best. The two common preservatives are alcohol and formalin. Rubbing alcohol (isopropyl) is suitable. Ethyl alcohol is generally sold in 95-percent strength and can be diluted to 60 to 70 percent. Commercial formaldehyde is usually 40 percent formalin and should be diluted to 5 percent formalin.

SHOULDER BAG, or knapsack, is very useful for carrying collecting gear, containers, first-aid kit, knife, pencil, notebook, and personal items.

AQUARIUMS provide an excellent place to study the habits and life histories of both plants and animals. Specimens may be kept for a long time if the aquarium is "balanced" in food, plants and animals.

NOTES AND LABELS give the specimens you collect their scientific value. In the field, you can make temporary labels with a pencil and place them in the vial or bottle with the specimens. Later the labels can be typed or printed carefully in a permanent ink. Always keep them with the specimens.

shoulder bag

label

belt with specimen vials

killing jar

PLANTS

Plants form the most conspicuous part of the pond, lake, and stream environment. Their role is highly important, for only plants can convert solar energy into chemical energy stored in food. Green plants—those containing chlorophyll pigments—do this in the process of photosynthesis, utilizing carbon dioxide, water, and light energy from the sun.

The simplest of the plants are the thallophytes, the group containing the bacteria, fungi, and algae (pp. 31-38). Many of these lower plants are single-celled and microscopic, but they sometimes occur in such abundance that they color the water and give it a distinctive odor. These smallest of the plants are the most important food producers in the aquatic environment. Filaments of algae that form the familiar pond scums usually harbor many microscopic animals.

Larger and slightly more complex in structure and life history are the bryophytes, the group containing liverworts and mosses (pp. 39-41). They grow abundantly in the moist soil along shores, and a few are aquatic.

Vascular plants, or tracheophytes, include the ferns (pp. 42-45) and the seed-bearing plants (pp. 46-73). These are the largest and most complex of all the plants. Ferns are most typical of moist shores, though a few species are aquatic. Some of the seed-bearing plants grow completely submerged. Others are rooted in the bottom, but their leaves or flowers may be on or above the surface. These plants offer protection and nesting sites to a variety of fishes and other animals; some are important foods of mammals, waterfowl, and turtles. Grasses, herbs, and shrubs rim the shore; trees form the crowning border.

ALGAE form pond scums and the green hairy growths on submerged objects in ponds and lakes. "Blooms" of diatoms may give the water a brownish color. The individual plants range in size from single cells to the mats of stoneworts resembling dense growths of higher plants. The single cells of some algae are joined together to form chains or filaments. Other single-celled algae swim like one-celled animals. Algae are found in all natural waters—even in hot springs. They contain chlorophyll and often other pigments.

Algae form the broad base on which the food pyramids in ponds and lakes are built. In manufacturing food, algae release oxygen, increasing the amount dissolved in the water. When overabundant, however, their decay may deplete the oxygen and cause "summerkill" of aquatic plants and animals.

MAJOR GROUPS OF FRESH-WATER ALGAE

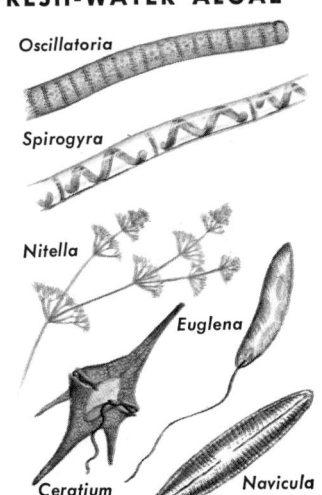

BLUE-GREEN ALGAE cells lack nuclei, and pigment is scattered. Slimy coating. Page 32.

Oscillatoria

Spirogyra

GREEN ALGAE cells have nuclei; pigments in distinct bodies. Most abundant pond algae. Page 34.

STONEWORTS are large green algae, brittle due to lime. Page 36.

Nitella

EUGLENOIDS, greenish or brownish cells, swim with flagellum. Have red eyespot. Page 36.

Euglena

DINOFLAGELLATES have one or more flagella. Free-swimming plants of open waters. Page 36.

DIATOMS are enclosed in two shells that fit together like a pillbox. Page 37.

Ceratium

Navicula

BLUE-GREEN ALGAE are simple, single-celled plants without a well-defined nucleus (the cell's control center). In addition to green chlorophyll, a blue and sometimes a red pigment are also present. The pigments are spread throughout the cell rather than in distinct bodies or plastids as in all other algae. In most kinds of blue-green algae the cells stick together to form slender strings, or filaments. They are most abundant in ponds containing much organic matter, hence the presence of rich growths of blue-green algae may be a clue to polluted waters. Such blooms are common in spring or summer, when conditions are favorable and the algae reach a population peak. An abundance of blue-green algae may give water a disagreeable odor or taste, and some make the water poisonous to animals that drink it.

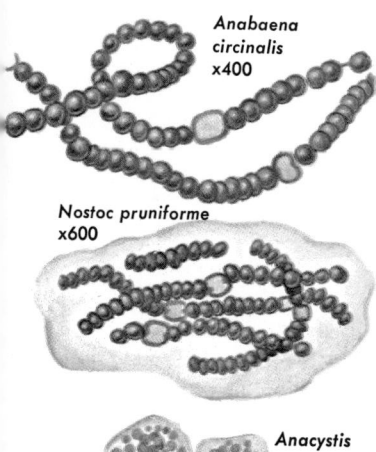

*Anabaena
circinalis
x400*

*Nostoc pruniforme
x600*

*Anacystis
cyanea
x500*

ANABAENA resembles a string of beads with larger empty cells scattered along the filament. Blooms of *Anabaena* are common, discoloring the water and giving it a putrid odor when the cells die and decay.

NOSTOC, similar to *Anabaena,* is enclosed in a gelatinous mass. Filaments may float or become attached to objects, living also in swift streams or on moist shores. In lakes, may grow in water 60 feet deep.

ANACYSTIS is a loose colony of small spherical green cells in a shapeless gelatinous mass. The colony floats in the water and is visible to the naked eye. Often found with *Anabaena.* May be poisonous to animals.

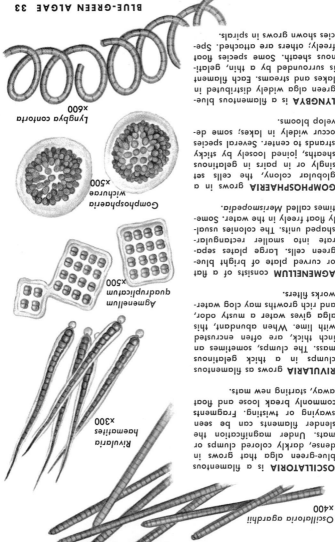

LYNGBYA is a filamentous blue-green alga widely distributed in lakes and streams. Each filament is surrounded by a thin, gelatinous sheath. Some species float freely; others are attached. Species shown grows in spirals.

Lyngbya contorta
x600

GOMPHOSPHAERIA grows in a globular colony, the cells set singly or in pairs in gelatinous sheaths, joined loosely by sticky strands to center. Several species occur widely in lakes; some develop blooms.

Gomphosphaeria wichurae
x500

AGMENELLUM consists of a flat or curved plate of bright blue-green cells. Large plates separate into smaller rectangular-shaped units. The colonies usually float freely in the water. Sometimes called Merismopedia.

Agmenellum quadruplicatum
x500

RIVULARIA grows as filamentous clumps in a thick gelatinous mass. The clumps, sometimes an inch thick, are often encrusted with lime. When abundant, this alga gives water a musty odor, and rich growths may clog waterworks filters.

Rivularia haematites
x300

OSCILLATORIA is a filamentous blue-green alga that grows in dense, darkly colored clumps or mats. Under magnification the slender filaments can be seen swaying or twisting. Fragments commonly break loose and float away, starting new mats.

Oscillatoria agardhii
x400

GREEN ALGAE are bright grass-green with pigments in special plastids, or chloroplasts. The cell has a well-defined nucleus. Green algae occur as single cells, as round and flattened colonies, and as filaments. Green algae are more abundant in ponds and lakes than all other algal groups combined. Some species are marine.

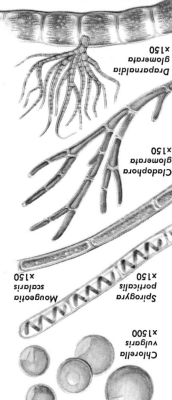

Draparnaldia
glomerata
x150

Cladophora
glomerata
x150

Mougeotia
scalaris
x150

Spirogyra
porticalis
x150

Chlorella
vulgaris
x1500

CHLORELLA, a single-celled green alga, may occur in clumps or loose aggregates or as solitary cells scattered among other algae. Widespread in N.A., especially in organically rich and polluted waters, giving them a musty odor.

SPIROGYRA is a common filamentous green alga with a spiral chloroplast in each cell. Frequently forms dense blankets on the surface of ponds in spring. In related Mougeotia, cells have a long platelike chloroplast that turns inside cell as it adjusts to intensity of sunlight.

CLADOPHORA has long, slim cells that form branching filaments. Some species grow attached; others float and may form tangled mats. Underwater currents may roll Cladophora into balls 3 to 4 inches in diameter. When its core decays, ball rises to the surface.

DRAPARNALDIA consists of barrel-shaped cells that form long strings, or filaments. The much-branched filaments bear tufts of smaller branches at intervals. Usually grows attached to rocks, sticks, or other objects.

VOLVOX forms large hollow spherical colonies of cells, each of which has an eyespot and two flagella. Some colonies consist of thousands of cells embedded in a gelatinous envelope from which the flagella protrude. In most species the cells are joined by strands of protoplasm. Daughter colonies form within the parent. As flagella beat, Volvox rotates and rolls through water.

DESMIDS are beautifully shaped, bright green cells common in plankton, especially in soft-water (low pH) lakes and bogs. The clear connection, or isthmus, between the two semicells is a characteristic of desmids. The cells of some desmids adhere end to end, forming filaments. Two common single-celled types are Micrasterias, divided into typical semicells, and Closterium, with cells usually crescent-shaped and with no isthmus.

SCENEDESMUS AND ANKISTRO- DESMUS, often found together, are particularly abundant in small ponds and pools. Ankistrodesmus is usually intermixed with other algae. Scenedesmus cells are smaller, and most species grow in colonies.

PEDIASTRUM AND HYDRODIC- TYON are closely related. Pediastrum, a common and wide-spread floating (planktonic) form, has many species. Hydrodictyon, or Water Net, forms flat sheets or cylindrical colonies several inches across. Both thrive in quiet waters.

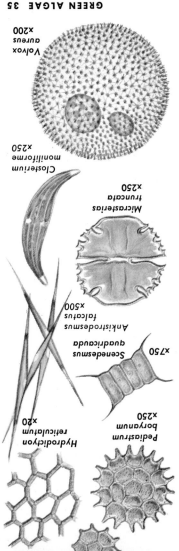

Volvox
aureus
x200

Closterium
moniliforme
x250

Micrasterias
truncata
x250

Ankistrodesmus
falcatus
x500

Scenedesmus
quadricauda
x750

Pediastrum
boryanum
x250

Hydrodictyon
reticulatum
x20

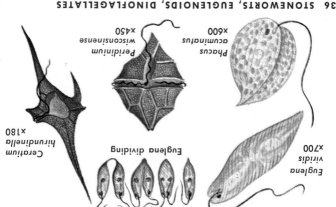

Ceratium
hirundinella
x180

Euglena dividing

Phacus
acuminatus
x600

Peridinium
wisconsinense
x450

Euglena
viridis
x700

STONEWORTS are green algae but are so much larger than others found in fresh water that they are sometimes classified in a group by themselves. Stoneworts grow best in hard water (high pH), often forming dense mats on the pond bottom. They usually have a garlic-like odor, and some species are covered with a thick, brittle limy crust. Both *Chara* and *Nitella* bear red reproductive structures at leaf nodes.

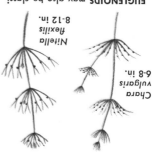

Chara
vulgaris
8-9 in.

Nitella
flexilis
8-12 in.

EUGLENOIDS may also be classified as animals because of their ability to move independently. Some species lack pigment and obtain food in animal fashion, but most have chlorophyll and manufacture their own food. *Euglena* is common in ponds rich in organic matter and may give the water a bright green color. It has a single flagellum and a conspicuous red eyespot. *Phacus* is very similar, but the cell is pear-shaped and less flexible.

DINOFLAGELLATES have two whiplike flagella. *Ceratium*, a common type, is spined and brownish in color. Its two flagella lie in a groove of the shell covering the single-celled plant. Most species are marine, but the one illustrated and *C. carolin-iana* live in ponds and lakes. *C. hirundinella* is common in plankton of hard-water lakes, often developing brown blooms. *Peridinium* is mainly marine; about 30 species in fresh water.

DIATOMS are microscopic, single-celled yellow-green algae. The two halves or "valves" of their cell overlap and fit together like the halves of a pillbox. The cell walls, of silica and pectin, may be finely sculptured with pits and lines. The fine lines are so perfectly formed that they are used for testing the focus of microscopes. Some species are common in plankton. These can move, propelled by a band of protoplasm streaming along a slit in the valve. Others cling to submerged objects or to one another in loose filaments.

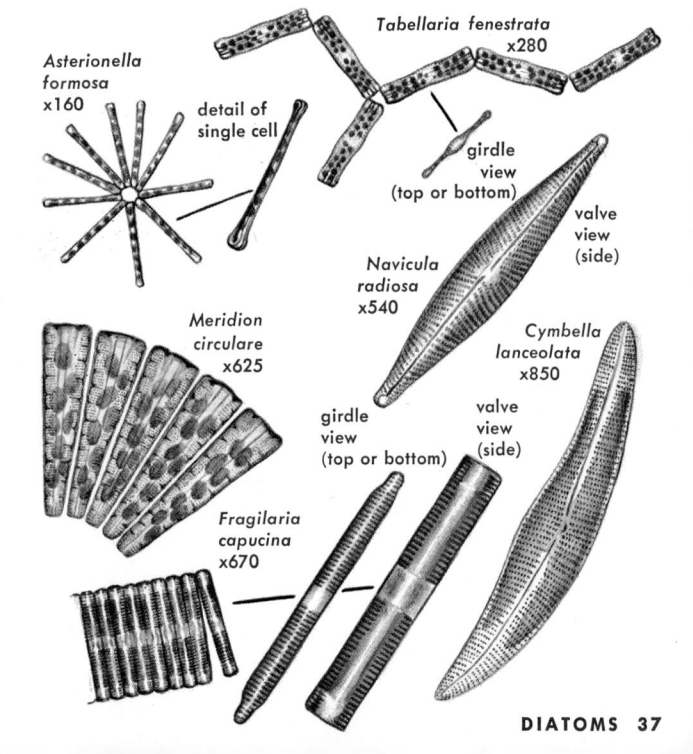

Tabellaria fenestrata
x280

Asterionella formosa
x160

detail of single cell

girdle view
(top or bottom)

valve view
(side)

Navicula radiosa
x540

Meridion circulare
x625

Cymbella lanceolata
x850

girdle view
(top or bottom)

valve view
(side)

Fragilaria capucina
x670

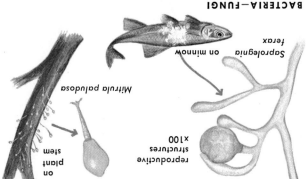

Saprolegnia ferax

on minnow

reproductive
structures
×100

Mirtula paludosa

on plant
stem

BACTERIA are microscopic, ranging from 1/25,000 to as small as 1/250,000 of an inch. Most kinds obtain their energy from dead plants and animals and thus are the principal agents of decay. They return such chemical nutrients as nitrogen, sulfur, and phosphorus to the pond or lake.

Bacteria are seldom abundant in waters with a high oxygen content, hence are rare in clear ponds or lakes. The filamentous types above live in water with a high hydrogen sulfide content (*Thiothrix*); in rich organic contamination (*Sphaerotilis*); and in a high iron content (*Leptothrix*).

AQUATIC FUNGI grow as parasites on living plants or animals and as saprophytes on those that are dead. Water molds (*Saprolegnia, Mirtula,* and others) are seen as whitish, fuzzy growths, the branching filaments spreading over and into wounds of fishes or other pond animals or on plants. In aquariums and hatcheries, these fungi also grow on fish eggs and may be difficult to control. The fuzzy filaments are reproductive structures. Spores are produced in great numbers and dispersed by water movements. They germinate and grow into new filaments.

Thiothrix sp. ×100   Sphaerotilus sp. ×500   Leptothrix sp. ×100

BRYOPHYTES (Mosses and Liverworts) grow in moist shady areas throughout the world. They are common in bogs and swamps, and in the humid tropics they often grow on trees. Great beds of liverworts and mosses usually develop on newly cleared ground. These rich carpets help to prevent soil erosion and hold moisture, thus paving the way for higher plants.

LIVERWORTS grow on moist soil and rocks along shores, and a few species live in water. The body, or thallus, of some liverworts is flat and lobed (liver-like); in others it is branched and leafy.

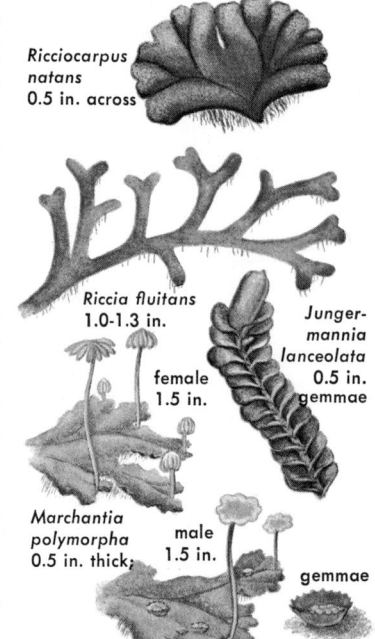

Ricciocarpus
natans
0.5 in. across

Riccia fluitans
1.0-1.3 in.

female
1.5 in.

Junger-
mannia
lanceolata
0.5 in.
gemmae

Marchantia
polymorpha
0.5 in. thick

male
1.5 in.

gemmae

RICCIOCARPUS often forms dense purple-green masses on pond surfaces. Each thallus is thick and lobed, with threadlike purplish scales below.

RICCIAS have many slender branches. When abundant, the plants may pile up in a green mass on shore or form a netlike sheet on the surface.

JUNGERMANNIA has leaflike parts arranged about a stem. Some species occur only in fast streams; others grow as emergent plants in quiet waters.

MARCHANTIA grows on moist shores. Male and female plants are separate. Sperm swim to the female and fertilize the egg, which then develops into a spore-producing stage. It remains parasitic on the female and releases spores that grow into new sexual-stage plants. *Marchantia* also produces buds, or gemmae, that grow into new plants.

MOSSES grow in dense mats, much like liverworts, but the flat leaflike structures of mosses grow from a central stalk. At times a spore case, usually on a long stem, grows from the leafy stalks. Spores ripen in the case and are released. Each spore that germinates becomes a leafy plant that reproduces sexually. The cycle is completed when a spore case is produced again.

SPHAGNUMS, or Peat Mosses, are the most familiar mosses of cool ponds and bogs. The numerous species grow in thick greenish mats along the edges and sometimes over the surface as a floating mat. A plant's leaves are dead near base of stalk but green and growing near tip. Leaves contain numerous empty cells with many holes in their walls. These cells may hold several times their weight in water, which is released slowly and keeps the moss moist even in dry weather.

Boat-leaved Sphagnum
S. palustre

Sharp-leaved
Sphagnum
S. capillaceum

water-holding
cells

The many species of sphagnums are identified by a variety of features. In one group the branches form rather thick tufts, and the walls of the empty cells are strengthened by spiral thickenings that are clearly visible as lines. In another group, the branches are slim and tapered, and the empty cells do not have

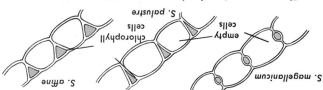

S. magellanicum

empty
cells

chlorophyll
cells

S. palustre

S. affine

spiral thickenings.

Another distinctive feature is the shape of the living cells, those that contain chlorophyll and hence are green. As shown above, the chlorophyll cells of *S. magellanicum* are elliptical. Those of *S. palustre* are narrowly triangular, but in *S. affine* the triangles are equilateral.

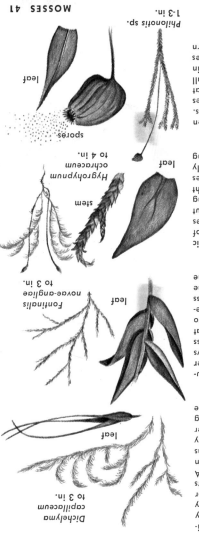

Philonotis sp.
1-3 in.

leaf

spores

Hygrohypnum
ochraceum
to 4 in.

leaf

stem

Fontinalis
novae-angliae
to 3 in.

leaf

leaf

Dichelyma
capillaceum
to 3 in.

WATER MOSS grows in cool climates. It is found most commonly as a tangled mat of feathery green filaments on submerged or on partially submerged objects along lake or pond shores. A variety of small animals live in these dense growths. The stems are slender and often highly branched, the tips usually lighter in color than the bases during the growing season. Spores are liberated in summer.

FOUNTAIN MOSS is found usually in fast-flowing, cold-water streams but occasionally grows in ponds. This dark-green moss occurs either as a waving mass attached to stones or other objects, lance-shaped leaves of Fountain Moss are densely clustered about the stalk except near its base. One of the largest of the mosses.

WATER HYPNUM is an aquatic form of Trailing Hypnum of damp woods. It grows on stones or in soil in bogs and ponds but is most abundant in fast-flowing streams. Leaves may be bright or very dark green. The leaves are arranged spirally and closely pressed about the stem, giving it a rather full appearance.

PHILONOTIS is a dark green moss of slow or stagnant waters. Its erect stems, about 2 inches long, often form a creeping mat on rocks or sand. Many small animals find food and cover in the matted moss. Spore capsules on long, slim stems. Plants turn 'hite when dry.

VASCULAR PLANTS (Tracheophytes) generally have roots, stems, and leaves with tubelike conducting tissues. One set of tissues (phloem) transfers manufactured food; another (xylem) conducts water up from the roots and also aids in supporting the plant. These features are adaptations to life on land, where most of the more than 250,000 vascular plants live. A few species are aquatic: that is, seeds germinate in water and plants grow submerged or are at least rooted in water.

Ferns and their relatives are commonly referred to as "lower vascular plants." The fern allies on this page grow in water or in very moist soils. On p. 43 are aqua-

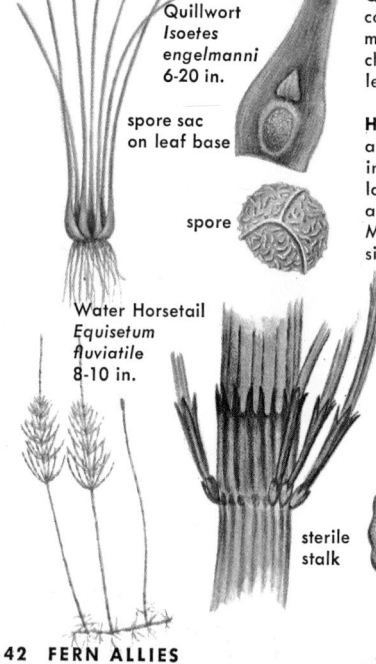

Quillwort
Isoetes engelmanni
6-20 in.

spore sac
on leaf base

spore

Water Horsetail
Equisetum fluviatile
8-10 in.

detail of branches

sterile stalk

hollow stem cross section

spore-bearing cone

fertile stalk

QUILLWORTS are fern allies common in shallow waters, wet meadows, and occasionally in clear lakes. The fleshy base of leaves is eaten by waterfowl.

HORSETAILS are fern allies. Of about 25 species, several grow in meadows and along pond and lake shores. The group flourished about 280 million years ago. Many have rough stems due to silica content.

tic ferns, followed on pp. 44-45 by wetland ferns. In ferns, the spore-producing (sporophyte) is the familiar plant. The sexual stage is inconspicuous.

"Higher vascular plants" bear seeds, flowers, and true roots. Those that grow in pond or lake waters or along the shore range in size from tiny pondweeds to giant cypresses. Some of the most common of these moist-area seed-bearers appear on pp. 46-73.

WATER SHAMROCKS are ferns of shallow waters. Their four clover-like leaflets, usually floating, rise on slender stalks from creeping stems rooted in the mud. Differences in the seedlike spore cases that develop near the leaf bases are useful in identifying species. *M. quadrifolia*, a native of Europe, grows in eastern states. *M. vestita* is also found locally in the East but is a western species, as are *M. macropoda* and *M. uncinata.*

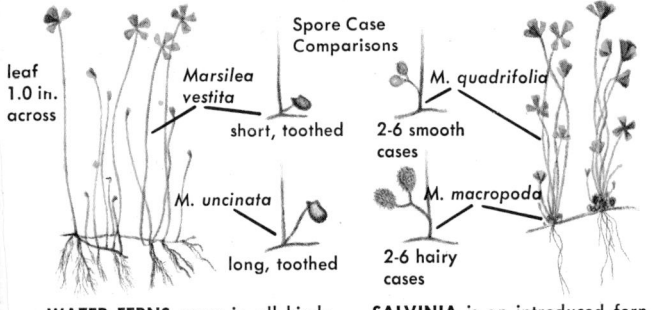

Spore Case
Comparisons

leaf
1.0 in.
across

*Marsilea
vestita*

short, toothed

M. uncinata

long, toothed

M. quadrifolia

2-6 smooth
cases

M. macropoda

2-6 hairy
cases

WATER FERNS occur in all kinds of quiet waters from coast to coast. Leaves lobed, scale-like. Form reddish-green mats. Reproduce by breaking apart.

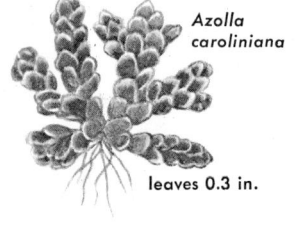

*Azolla
caroliniana*

leaves 0.3 in.

SALVINIA is an introduced fern, mostly of warmer regions. Leaves have pimple-like swellings and stiff hairs on the upper surface. Submerged leaves are rootlike.

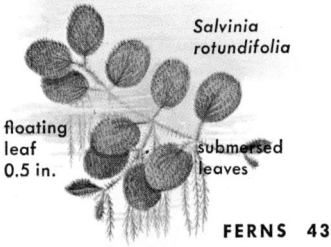

*Salvinia
rotundifolia*

floating
leaf
0.5 in.

submersed
leaves

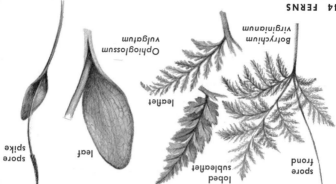

Botrychium virginianum

spore frond

lobed subleaflet

leaflet

Ophioglossum vulgatum

spore spike

leaf

RATTLESNAKE FERN has triangular lacy fronds. Spore cases containing yellow spores are borne on a separate stem. Common in wetlands and along shores of woodland ponds, particularly in acid, shaded soils. Commonly to 2 feet tall, often taller.

ADDER'S TONGUE FERNS, 4 to 15 inches tall, inhabit wet fields and lake shores throughout N.A. Their single leaf, about halfway up stalk, is spoon-shaped. Spores are borne at tip of a slender stalk rising above the leaf. Related to Rattlesnake Ferns.

CRESTED WOODFERN is a lacy evergreen fern of low, wet woods and marshes. Grows in rounded clusters from rootstock. Similar Spinulose Fern also common along ponds, grows in short rows. Both 2 feet tall.

MARSH FERN, with thin, delicate leaves, grows about 2.5 feet tall. Very sensitive to frost. Common from central N.A. eastward, especially in wet meadows. Leaflets opposite at base, becoming alternate toward tip.

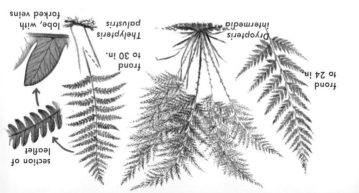

Dryopteris intermedia

frond to 24 in.

Thelypteris palustris

frond to 30 in.

lobe, with forked veins

section of leaflet

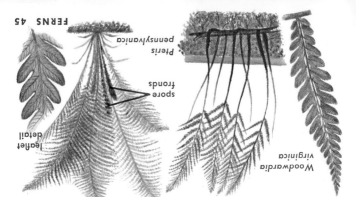

Pteris pennsylvanica

spore fronds

leaflet detail

Woodwardia virginica

CINNAMON FERN, common in eastern N.A., has twice-divided, narrow sterile fronds about 3 feet tall. Spore stalks, appearing in early spring, are at first green, then cinnamon. Leafstalk base hairy.

VIRGINIA CHAIN FERN grows in acid bogs, swamps, and wetlands of central and eastern N.A. The leaves, about 3-4 feet tall, arise from scaly rootstalks that wind through the soil. Double rows of spore cases are found on underside of leaflets.

ROYAL FERN occurs widely from Mexico into Canada in wet soils, marshes, and even in shallow waters of ponds. Leaves are twice-divided and may be 6 feet tall, with light brown spore cases at tips.

OSTRICH FERN is one of the largest N.A. ferns, with sterile fronds up to 5 feet tall. Spore-bearing fronds, nearly 2 feet tall, are dark, hard, and pod-like. Widely distributed in central and eastern N.A. in swamps and along lake shores.

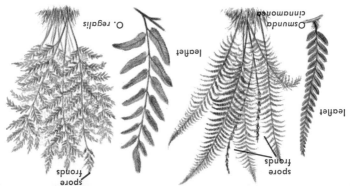

Osmunda cinnamomea

leaflet

spore fronds

O. regalis

leaflet

spore fronds

CATTAILS, first of the flowering plants treated in this book, are common in marshes and ditches and along shallows of lakes, ponds, and slow streams. The long slender leaves reach a height of 6 to 8 feet. The flower stems, usually shorter than the leaves, bear two masses of flower parts. Cattails spread by their wind-borne seeds and also by their starchy underground root-stocks. Twelve species occur in N.A.

BROAD-LEAVED CATTAIL is found through most of N.A. Upper flower cluster of male (staminate) flowers and lower cluster of female (pistillate) flowers are closely joined on the cattail. Stem sturdy, leaves flat.

NARROW-LEAVED CATTAIL occurs in eastern N.A., growing in both fresh and brackish waters. Male and female flower clusters are well separated on flower spike. Stem is slender, the leaves rounded.

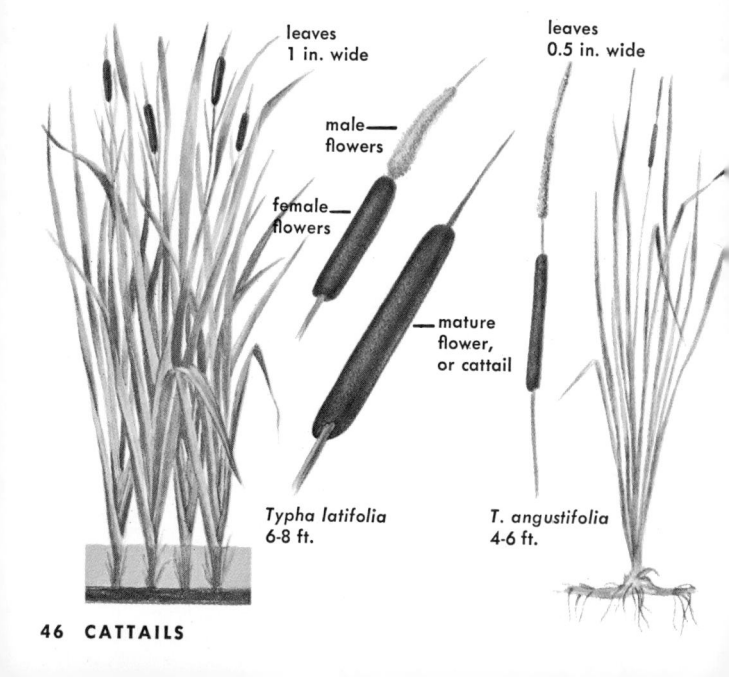

leaves 1 in. wide

male flowers

female flowers

mature flower, or cattail

Typha latifolia 6-8 ft.

leaves 0.5 in. wide

T. angustifolia 4-6 ft.

BUR-REEDS grow in wet soil or in shallow waters, commonly with cattails, to which they are closely related. The two are frequently the dominant plants in the marshy borders of ponds. Bur-reeds have long slender leaves. Their seeds are borne on separate stalks in dense bur-like clusters. About 10 species occur in N.A., mainly in central and northern areas. Seeds eaten by waterfowl; seeds and leaves by muskrats.

GIANT BUR-REED, 3 to 6 feet tall, is widely distributed in N.A. It flowers in early summer. The large clusters of female flowers are located below smaller male clusters on same stem. Straplike leaves float on surface.

WESTERN BUR-REED, smaller than Giant Bur-reed, is common from the northern Rockies to the Pacific and also in New England. Insect larvae and other small animals live on underwater stems.

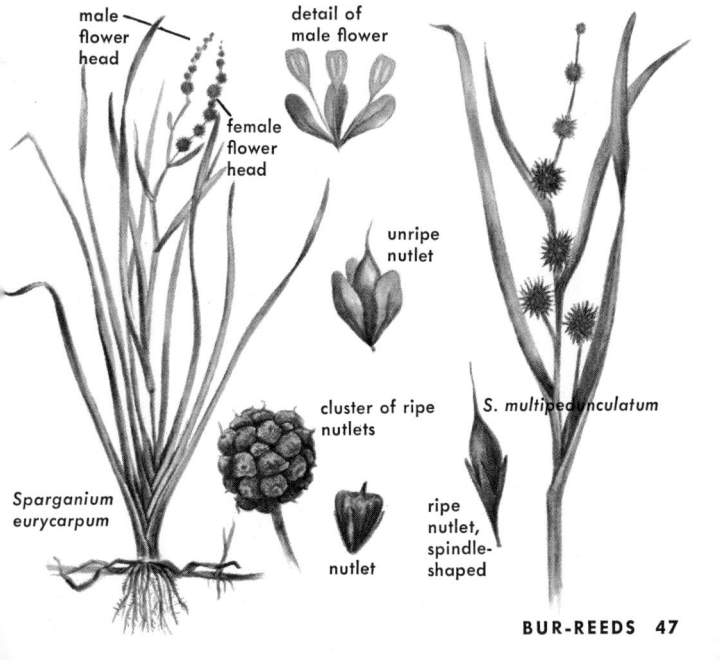

male flower head

detail of male flower

female flower head

unripe nutlet

cluster of ripe nutlets

S. multipedunculatum

Sparganium eurycarpum

nutlet

ripe nutlet, spindle-shaped

PONDWEEDS are the largest family of truly aquatic seed plants. They are perennials, growing mainly in cool regions. More than 60 species grow in fresh-water ponds and lakes and some even in brackish and salt water. Several kinds of ducks feed almost wholly on pondweeds. The dense underwater growths of pondweeds provide cover for fishes, snails, and other animals. Pondweeds survive the winter by using food stored in their underground stems and tubers. Tubers also break off and grow into new plants. In summer, heavy growths of some pondweeds may interfere with boating, fishing, and swimming. Most fresh-water pondweeds have spike-like flowers; leaves usually alternate along the stem.

LEAFY PONDWEED is found in clear ponds and streams of northern N.A. Its leaves, all submersed, are thin and tapelike with flower spikes in axils. Fruit keeled.

BERCHTOLD'S PONDWEED is common in northeastern and central N.A. Both floating and submerged leaves are slender.

CRISP PONDWEED, introduced from Europe, is widespread in eastern and central N.A. Grows in clear and polluted waters, sometimes at depths of 5 feet. Crinkled, rather broad leaves are submerged; alternate on lower stem, clustered and opposite near tip. Fruit beaked.

VARIABLE PONDWEED has broad, rather elliptical floating leaves and somewhat narrower submerged leaves. Widespread in temperate N.A. waters.

FLOATING BROWNLEAF has broadly rounded floating leaves and long, ribbon-like, submerged leaves. Fruit with almost no keel. It grows in quiet waters throughout N.A.

SAGO PONDWEED is widespread in N.A. in hard-water and brackish lakes, ponds, and sluggish streams. The stems are many-branched, and the leaves are slender. Because its tubers and seeds are a highly prized waterfowl food, Sago Pondweed has been widely planted.

HORNED PONDWEED occurs in ponds, lakes, canals, and brackish waters from coast to coast. Unlike those of other pondweeds, the Horned Pondweed's slim leaves are arranged opposite on the slender stem. Flattened fruit, or nutlet, has teeth along its outer margin. Nutlets sometimes eaten by waterfowl.

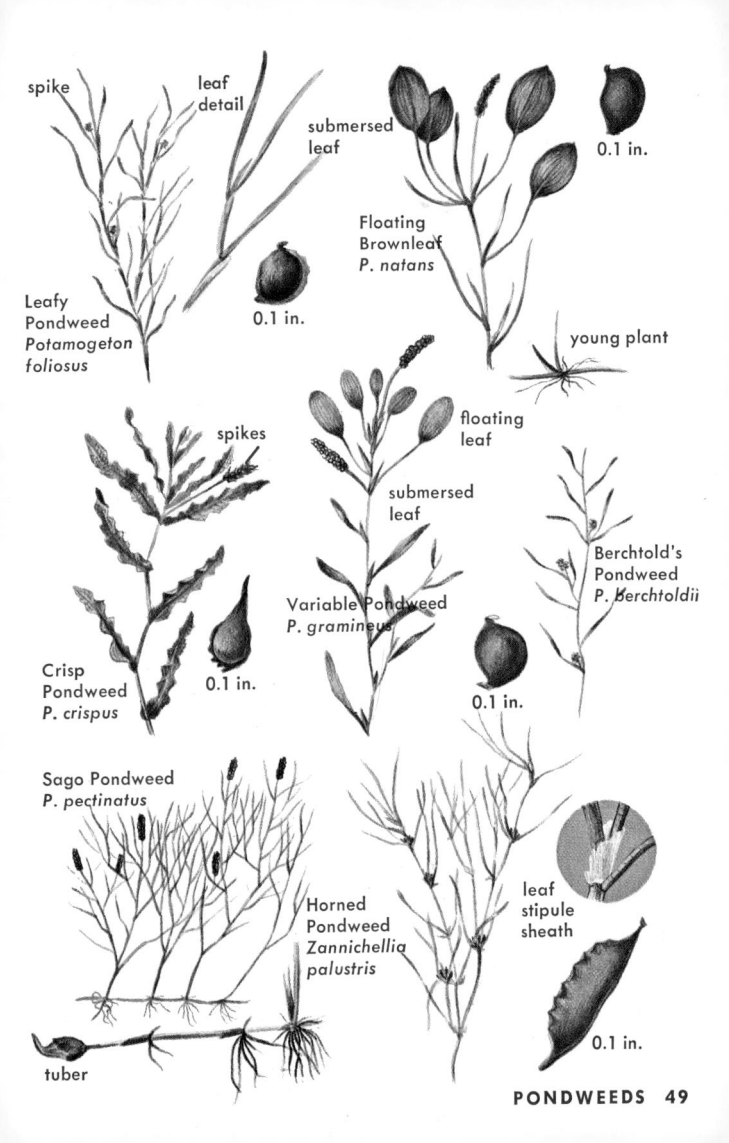

spike

leaf detail

submersed leaf

0.1 in.

Floating Brownleaf
P. natans

Leafy Pondweed
Potamogeton foliosus

0.1 in.

spikes

young plant

floating leaf

submersed leaf

Berchtold's Pondweed
P. berchtoldii

Crisp Pondweed
P. crispus

0.1 in.

Variable Pondweed
P. gramineus

0.1 in.

Sago Pondweed
P. pectinatus

Horned Pondweed
Zannichellia palustris

leaf stipule sheath

tuber

0.1 in.

PONDWEEDS 49

NAIADS, often called Waterweeds, typically grow submerged. Their slender leaves are swollen at base and form whorls along the stems. About 35 species are known in temperate and tropical regions, but only 8 occur in N.A., most abundantly in eastern states. Stems, leaves, and seeds are a favorite food of ducks. Plants provide shelter for many small aquatic animals.

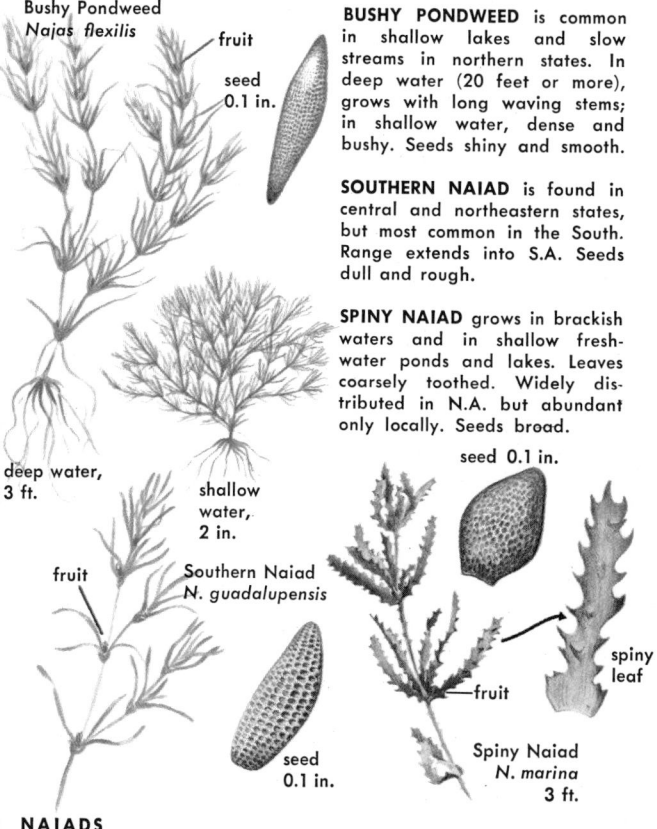

Bushy Pondweed
Najas flexilis

fruit

seed
0.1 in.

deep water,
3 ft.

shallow
water,
2 in.

fruit

Southern Naiad
N. guadalupensis

seed
0.1 in.

seed 0.1 in.

fruit

spiny
leaf

Spiny Naiad
N. marina
3 ft.

BUSHY PONDWEED is common in shallow lakes and slow streams in northern states. In deep water (20 feet or more), grows with long waving stems; in shallow water, dense and bushy. Seeds shiny and smooth.

SOUTHERN NAIAD is found in central and northeastern states, but most common in the South. Range extends into S.A. Seeds dull and rough.

SPINY NAIAD grows in brackish waters and in shallow freshwater ponds and lakes. Leaves coarsely toothed. Widely distributed in N.A. but abundant only locally. Seeds broad.

WATER PLANTAINS include Arrowheads, or Duck Potatoes, which usually have edible tubers. The leaves arise in bunches from a basal stalk and may be egg-shaped, slender, or arrow-shaped. Flowers, which have 3 petals, are borne on long slender stems. About 50 species in N.A. Some are emergent; others grow submerged in shallow water.

WATER PLANTAIN grows in wet areas from Canada southward. The broadly ovate leaves are coarsely veined. Pinkish or white flowers are at ends of stiff stems rising above leaves.

DUCK POTATO grows in shallow shore zones of all quiet waters in N.A. except in the Southwest. Length and shape of leaf blades varies with depth of water. Widely planted; thick tubers a favorite waterfowl food.

GRASSY ARROWHEAD is common in ponds and along streams of eastern N.A. The leaves vary in shape — broad in shallow water, narrow in deep.

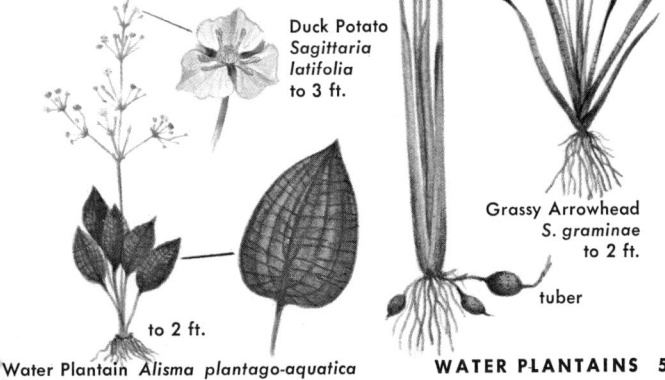

Duck Potato
Sagittaria latifolia
to 3 ft.

Grassy Arrowhead
S. graminae
to 2 ft.

tuber

to 2 ft.

Water Plantain *Alisma plantago-aquatica*

TRUE GRASSES include only a few aquatic species, difficult to identify. Their two-ranked (2 rows on stem), parallel-veined leaves have sheaths loosely encircling round hollow stems. Flowers in spikelets.

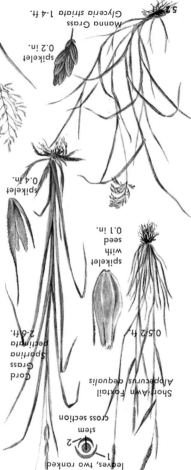

SHORT-AWN FOXTAIL, found throughout N.A. except in the southern states, grows in shallow ponds, ditches, or wet areas periodically dry. Sometimes trails over surface of ponds. Spikelets in a slim, dense cluster.

CORD GRASS has straight stems and long strong leaves. It grows in shallow water along lakes where its roots bind the sand. Also grows in marshes except in Southeast. Spikelets in two rows up spike.

MANNA GRASSES are perennial plants with tall stems growing from rhizomes, or rooted stems. About 10 species are known in N.A., where they are most abundant in the East.

CUT GRASS has feathery masses of seed clusters and finely sawtoothed leaves. Common in shallow waters and wet areas, where it may grow in dense patches. Widespread in N.A.

Short-Awn Foxtail
Alopecurus aequalis
0.55 ft.

Cord Grass
Spartina pectinata
2-6 ft.

spikelet with seed 0.1 in.

stem cross section

leaves, two ranked
1
2

spikelet 0.2 in.

Manna Grass
Glyceria striata 1-4 ft.

rootstock

Cut Grass
Leersia oryzoide
2-4 ft.

spikelet

spikelet 0.4 in.

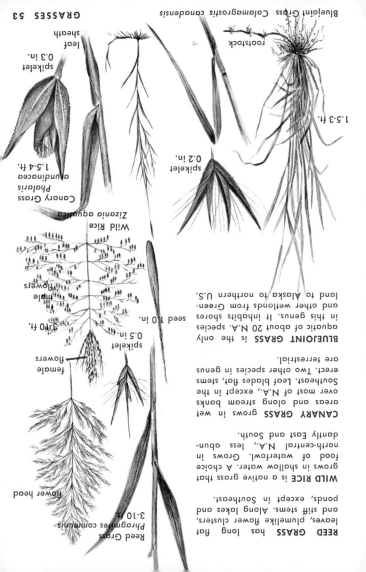

Bluejoint Grass *Calamagrostis canadensis*

rootstock

1.5–3 ft.

spikelet 0.2 in.

BLUEJOINT GRASS is the only aquatic of about 20 N.A. species in this genus. It inhabits shores and other wetlands from Greenland to Alaska to northern U.S.

leaf sheath

spikelet 0.3 in.

Canary Grass *Phalaris arundinacea* 1.5–4 ft.

Wild Rice *Zizania aquatica*

male flowers

3–10 ft.

seed 1.0 in.

spikelet 0.5 in.

female flowers

flower head

Reed Grass *Phragmites communis* 3–10 ft.

REED GRASS has long flat leaves, plumelike flower clusters, and stiff stems. Along lakes and ponds, except in Southeast.

WILD RICE is a native grass that grows in shallow water. A choice food of waterfowl. Grows in north-central N.A., less abundantly East and South.

CANARY GRASS grows in wet areas and along stream banks over most of N.A., except in the Southeast. Leaf blades flat, stems erect. Two other species in genus are terrestrial.

SEDGES are grasslike plants with three-ranked leaves (3 rows on stem). The basal sheath of each leaf grows tightly around the solid stem, which is triangular in cross section. Many of the approximately 3,000 species in this family grow in water or in wetlands.

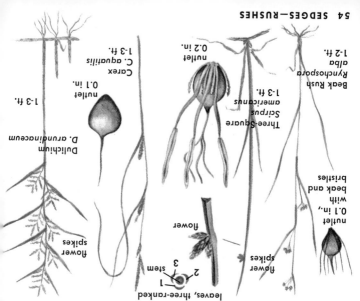

CAREX (about 1,000 species) are widely distributed sedges of quiet waters, marshes, and wet meadows in temperate regions. Seed clusters, or nutlets, grow closely to the three-sided stems.

DULICHIUM has short leaves and, unlike most sedges, a hollow stem. It grows in bogs and along marshy shores of quiet waters of the East Coast, in northern states, and in the Pacific Northwest.

BEAK RUSHES (about 200 species) are perennials found mainly in warm regions. Species shown is common in north-central and eastern states, rarely in Northwest. Ducks eat nutlets.

THREE-SQUARE, also known as the Chair-makers' Rush, is one of about 150 bulrushes. It has densely packed seed clusters and short leaves arising near base of stem. Grows in shallows of coastal and inland waters.

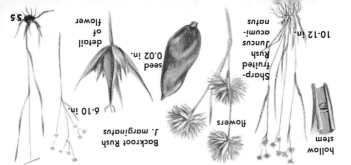

Backroot Rush
J. marginatus
6-10 in.

detail of flower

seed 0.02 in.

55

flowers

Sharp-fruited Rush
Juncus acuminatus
10-12 in.

hollow stem

SHARP-FRUITED RUSH has cylindrical leaves and a projection on tip of seed. Widespread in eastern N.A.

BLACKROOT RUSH grows in shallows and along shores in central and eastern N.A. Rootstock stout and black.

RUSHES are emergent plants with flattened, often hollow leaves. The stems are also hollow or pith-filled. Flowers are borne in clusters on or near tip of stem. Grow in shallow fresh water and in salt marshes. Genus contains about 200 species, difficult to distinguish.

SPIKE RUSHES (about 150 species) grow in marshes and along shores. Stems, mainly leafless, and seed clusters arise in a clump from matted rootstock. Water Chestnut, native to China, is a tuber of a spike rush.

SAW GRASS, to about 10 feet tall, grows in fresh and brackish water and in wetlands of the southeastern coastal plains including the Gulf. Characteristic of Florida's Everglades. Leaves have sharp, spiny edges.

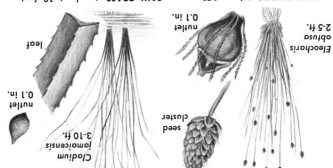

Eleocharis obtusa
2-5 ft.

nutlet 0.1 in.

seed cluster

Cladium jamaicensis
3-10 ft.

leaf

nutlet 0.1 in.

ARUMS of about 1,500 species are mainly moist-soil land plants of the tropics and temperate regions. Skunk Cabbage, Jack-in-the-pulpit, and the economically important Taro are arums. Arums have small flowers clustered tightly on a spikelike stalk. Leaves are large and net-veined. Stems are thick; roots, tuberous.

ARROW ARUM has large, fleshy, arrowhead-shaped leaves. The flower mass and fruits are greenish. Grows in shallow waters and on wet shores in central and eastern N.A. Do not confuse with Duck Potato (p. 51).

WATER LETTUCE, a widespread, warm-climate species, is found in ditches, slow streams, and ponds in southeastern U.S. Its bright-green, fleshy leaves grow as rosettes. New plants bud from the basal stems.

SWEET FLAG grows from the Mississippi Basin eastward to the Atlantic Coast. Spreads by a creeping rootstock, which is thick and pungent.

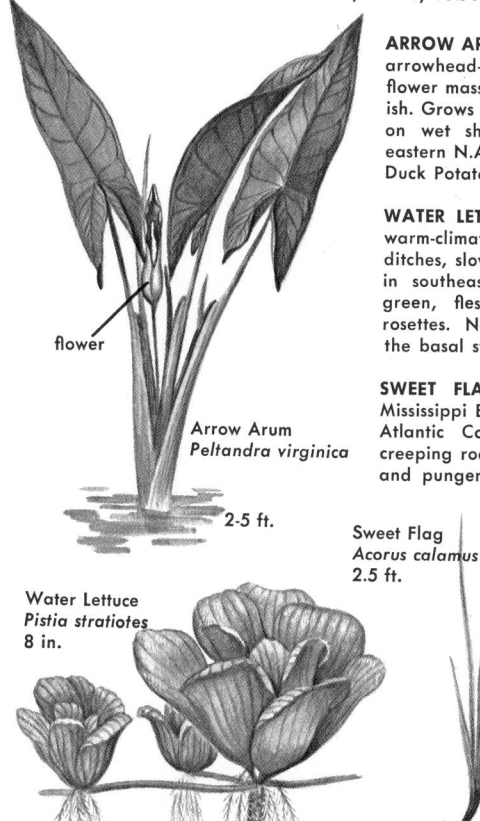

flower

Arrow Arum
Peltandra virginica

2-5 ft.

Sweet Flag
Acorus calamus
2.5 ft.

Water Lettuce
Pistia stratiotes
8 in.

rootstock

DUCKWEEDS, tiny floating herbs, are a favorite food of waterfowl. About 25 species of these smallest of the seed plants are known. Tiny flowers, rarely produced, grow out of the leaflike body, which lacks true leaves and stems. Reproduction is mainly vegetative, by a division of the plant body.

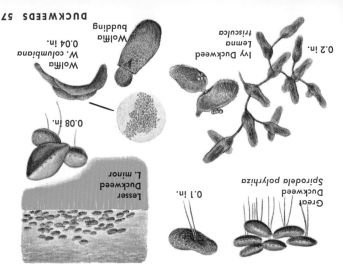

Wolffia budding

Wolffia
W. columbiana
0.04 in.

Ivy Duckweed
Lemna
trisulca
0.2 in.

0.08 in.

Lesser
Duckweed
L. minor

Great
Duckweed
Spirodela polyrhiza

0.1 in.

GREAT DUCKWEED has several rootlets beneath plant body, and undersurface is frequently purplish. It grows in quiet waters and sluggish streams throughout N.A., sometimes forming dense mats on the surface.

IVY DUCKWEED plants often interlock, their leaflike bodies joined to form lattice-like sheets on the surface or just beneath. Plants may lack roots. Ivy Duckweed is widespread in N.A., except in the South.

LESSER DUCKWEED has a single rootlet hanging below plant body. It is common in ponds and slow streams throughout much of N.A., like Great Duckweed, it often forms floating mats that cover a pond's surface.

WOLFFIA is thick, granular, and lacks rootlets. It is thought to be the smallest seed plant. Often occurs with Water Fern (p. 43) and Lesser Duckweed in quiet waters from the Mississippi Valley eastward.

PICKERELWEEDS form a varied family found mainly in warm regions. Some have free-floating, broad leaves; others have slender leaves and grow rooted in the mud, either submerged or emergent. The flowers are showy. Pickerelweeds are commonly the first plants on the new land as a pond fills with sediments.

MUD PLANTAIN is more tolerant of cold than most pickerelweeds. It grows in shallow ponds and sluggish streams on the Pacific Coast and in central and eastern N.A. Blooms summer and autumn. Stems may trail many feet.

PICKERELWEED grows in shallow water and along muddy shores from the Mississippi eastward to Nova Scotia. Its flowers are borne on a spike. Several other species differ in shape of leaves. One species has white flowers.

WATER HYACINTH, introduced from S.A., is a floating plant with broad leaves and swollen, air-filled leaf stalks. The blue or white flowers grow in erect clusters. Water Hyacinths grow in streams and quiet waters in the South. Dense, feathery roots harbor a rich association of small animals; broad leaves shade bottom plants and animals. Dense growths can block a stream.

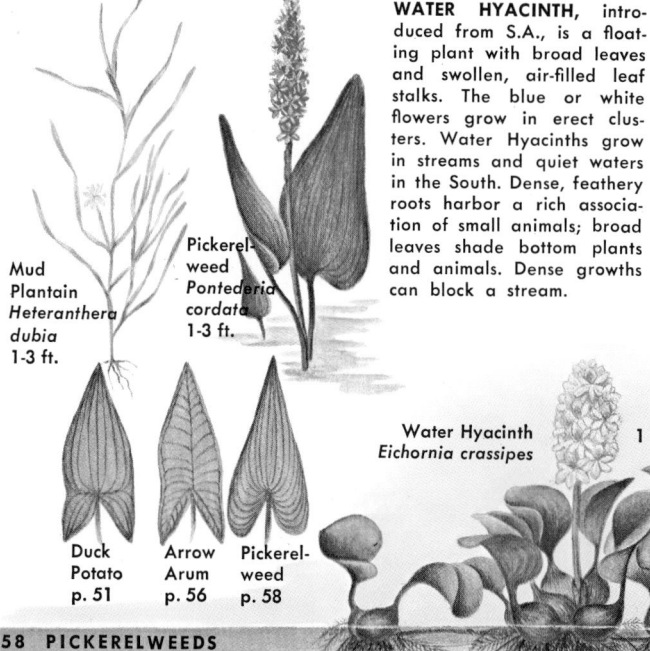

Mud Plantain
Heteranthera dubia
1-3 ft.

Pickerel-
weed
Pontederia cordata
1-3 ft.

Duck
Potato
p. 51

Arrow
Arum
p. 56

Pickerel-
weed
p. 58

Water Hyacinth
Eichornia crassipes
1 ft.

SMARTWEEDS include only a few aquatics in the more than 250 N.A. species forming the genus.

WATER SMARTWEED, a wide-spread species, has glossy leaves and spikes of greenish-white flowers along slender stems.

AMPHIBIOUS SMARTWEED, of northern U.S. and southern Canada, has clusters of pink flowers. Seeds of both are wildlife food.

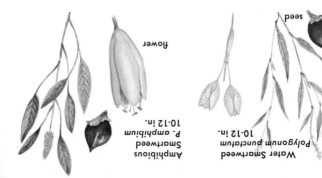

Water Smartweed
Polygonum punctatum
10-12 in.

seed

Amphibious Smartweed
P. amphibium
10-12 in.

flower

WATERWEED, FROGBIT, AND WILD CELERY leaves are in whorls or emerge from rootstock in a cluster.

WATERWEED is common in many ponds and also sluggish streams of the Northeast and Midwest. In favorable habitats it forms dense masses. The closely related *Elodea,* introduced from South America, is used in aquariums.

FROGBIT is found mostly in quiet, mud-bottomed waters in the Southeast and in the Mississippi Valley. May grow as a floating or as a rooted plant.

WILD CELERY grows in eastern N.A. The thick, fleshy stems are a favorite waterfowl food. After the floating flower is pollinated, a threadlike stem pulls it underwater, where fruit then ripens.

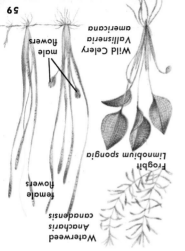

Waterweed
Anacharis canadensis

Frogbit
Limnobium spongia

Wild Celery
Vallisneria americana

female flowers

male flowers

WATER LILIES

WATER LILIES of more than 100 species are widely distributed in shallow ponds and slow rivers from the tropics through temperate areas. They grow from thick, branching rootstocks. Some are small, but many kinds have showy pink, yellow, or white flowers and large, flat, floating leaves that may cover a pond's surface. Many small aquatic animals lay their eggs on the leaves and stems of water lilies.

WATER SHIELD, common in central and eastern N.A., has small floating leaves. Its stems and the underside of its leaves have a gelatinous coating. Often eaten by ducks.

YELLOW WATER LILY, or Cow Lily, is common throughout central and eastern N.A. It grows from the muddy bottoms of ponds and streams, often with White Water Lily. The rootstock is stout. The notched leaves are round to heart-shaped.

WHITE WATER LILY occurs in streams, ponds, and lakes in the upper Mississippi Valley and Great Lakes regions. Unlike other water lilies, it has little scent. Its leaves are not purplish underneath. Flowers open in the morning and usually close by midafternoon. Rootstock and seeds eaten by wildlife.

LITTLE WATER LILY grows in Great Lakes region and in New England. The attractive flowers are seldom more than an inch in diameter. Grows in deeper water than most water lilies. More common in lakes than in ponds.

LOTUS, widely distributed in eastern N.A., has wide leaves and large, yellow flowers. Its long stems branch from thick, tuber-like roots. Indians ate the seeds and tubers.

SCENTED POND LILY has large, notched, rounded leaves, dark green on the upper surface and reddish-purple below. The pink or white flowers have a rich, sweet fragrance. Scented Pond Lily has a wider range than White Water Lily.

FANWORT has a slender stem covered with a jellylike slime. Though a member of the water lily family, the whitish or yellowish flowers are small. Fanwort occurs from the Mississippi Valley eastward. Dense growths harbor many small animals. Fanwort is a popular aquarium plant, and has been widely introduced.

WESTERN WATER LILY inhabits ponds, slow-flowing streams, and shallow lakes from the Rockies to northern California. This species has 9 sepals surrounding its petals; most water lilies have 6 sepals.

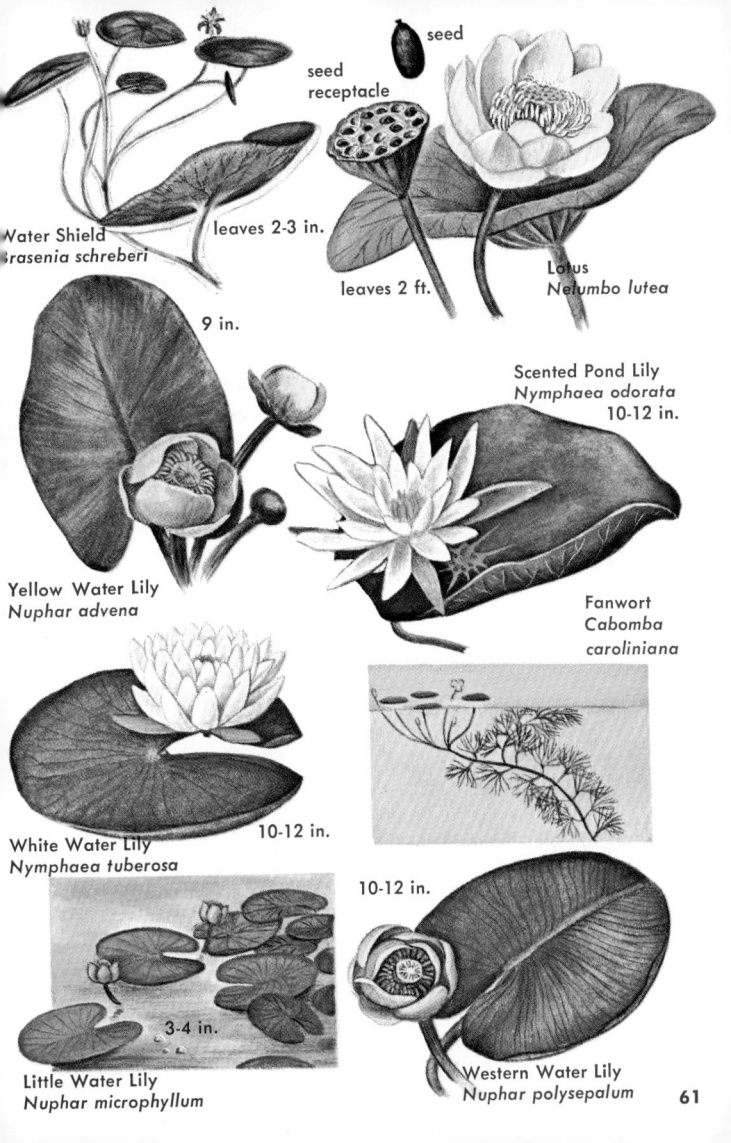

Water Shield
Brasenia schreberi

leaves 2-3 in.

seed

seed
receptacle

leaves 2 ft.

Lotus
Nelumbo lutea

9 in.

Scented Pond Lily
Nymphaea odorata
10-12 in.

Yellow Water Lily
Nuphar advena

Fanwort
*Cabomba
caroliniana*

White Water Lily
Nymphaea tuberosa

10-12 in.

10-12 in.

3-4 in.

Little Water Lily
Nuphar microphyllum

Western Water Lily
Nuphar polysepalum

61

OTHER POND AND SHORE PLANTS, representing more than a dozen different families, vary in size, color, and form, but all add to the richness of the shallows and shores of ponds and lakes. Shore plants provide cover and nesting sites for mammals, birds, reptiles, and many kinds of invertebrates. Only a few of these herbaceous and woody plants can be shown here. See also the Golden Nature Guides *Trees, Flowers,* and *Seashores,* and the Golden Regional Guides for additional plants of lakes, ponds, and wetlands.

Water Cress
Nasturtium officinale

12 in.

18-24 in.

Alligator Weed
Alternanthera philoxeroides

Glasswort
Salicornia rubra

8-12 in.

flowering spike

WATER CRESS (mustard family) was introduced from Europe. It grows in cold, spring-fed ponds and streams, often forming dense mats. The sprawling stems commonly take root where they touch the mud. Compound leaves bear 3 to 11 roundish leaflets, largest at tip. Seeds in slim pods. Used in salads or as a garnish.

ALLIGATOR WEED, a low-growing, creeping plant of southeastern U.S., occurs commonly in ponds and ditches. In Louisiana it chokes bayous, making boating difficult. Stems creeping, often taking root at nodes. The lance-shaped leaves are opposite. Flowers are borne in small dense clusters or heads.

GLASSWORTS are plants of brackish coastal waters and inland alkaline lakes and ponds. One species is found on salt flats and along shores of ponds in the Rockies. The leaves are small and scalelike; the stems soft and jointed; branches opposite. The small flowers are embedded in the thick stems.

HORNWORT, or Coontail, grows beneath the surface in quiet waters throughout N.A. Its branched leaves, brittle and crowded toward tip, are arranged in whorls around a slender stem. Hornwort's flowers are pollinated underwater. The seeds, eaten by waterfowl, have a tough covering.

YELLOW WATER CROWFOOT, a buttercup, grows on muddy areas or in temporary ponds in cooler parts of N.A. Its floating leaves are broad and three-lobed; the submersed leaves are finely branched. Both the nutlets and leaves are eaten by wildlife. Several other yellow buttercups are also aquatics.

WHITE WATER CROWFOOT, also a buttercup, occurs widely in N.A. except in southern states. It grows in shallow ponds and streams. Its weak, flexible stems sometimes forming thick entanglements. The finely branched leaves are usually submersed. Nutlet is distinctly beaked; small emergent flowers are white.

Hornwort
Ceratophyllum demersum
stems 6-10 ft.

leaf detail,
showing teeth

Yellow Water
Crowfoot
Ranunculus pursii
nutlet 0.1 in.
1-1.5 ft.

flower

White Water
Crowfoot
R. longirostris
nutlet 0.1 in.
1-1.5 ft.

COMPARISON OF PLANTS WITH FINELY BRANCHED LEAVES

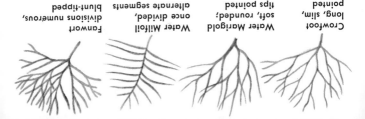

Crowfoot
long, slim,
pointed

Water Marigold
soft, rounded;
tips pointed

Water Milfoil
once divided,
alternate segments

Fanwort
divisions numerous,
blunt-tipped

MERMAID WEEDS (water milfoil family) are common in quiet waters of eastern N.A. Leaves near base of stem notched; those above are not. Three species.

ERYNGO, related to Water Parsnip, grows along shores from New Jersey southward along Atlantic and Gulf coasts. Also called Button Snakeroot. Flowers in dense heads.

BLADDERWORTS (bladderwort family) are most abundant in tropical waters, but about a dozen species grow in central and eastern N.A. Some bear on their branches tiny bladders in which small animals are trapped.

WATER HEMLOCK, also called Spotted Cowbane, is a common member of the parsley family growing in wet soils throughout N.A. Blooms from June through September; its numerous white flowers borne in a dense head. Roots, which resemble sweet potatoes and smell like parsnips, are poisonous, as are stems.

BLUE FLAG, an iris, grows in wetlands and along shores throughout central and eastern N.A. The sepals of the showy, usually violet-blue flowers are larger than the petals. Blooms in May and June. The flowers to 4 inches across.

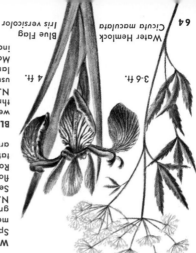

Mermaid Weed
Proserpinaca palustris

flower

10-12 in.

2 ft.

Eryngo
Eryngium aquaticum

Bladderwort
Utricularia vulgaris

bladder

Water Hemlock
Cicuta maculata

3-6 ft.

Blue Flag
Iris versicolor

4 ft.

64

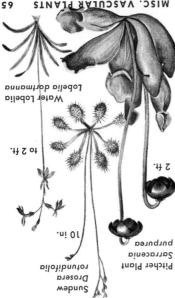

WATER LOBELIA, the only strictly aquatic lobelia, has a milky juice and light violet tubular flowers with flaring tips. The flowers may extend above surface or be submerged. Leaves form a rosette. Central N.A.

Water Lobelia
Lobelia dortmanna

to 2 ft.

2 ft.

to 10 in.

PITCHER PLANTS have hollow leaves, shaped like a pitcher or a trumpet, which contain a liquid consisting of rainwater and a fluid from the plant. Insects are drowned in the fluid and absorbed ("digested") by the plant. Pitcher plants grow in bogs and wet soils in eastern N.A. and in California.

Pitcher Plant
Sarracenia purpurea

SUNDEW is a low-growing herb found in bogs and wet areas throughout N.A. Insects are attracted to and caught in sweet, sticky liquid secreted by rosette of hairy, flat leaves.

Sundew
Drosera rotundifolia

WATER MILFOIL (water milfoil family) is widespread in quiet waters and slow streams in most of N.A. Its small purplish flowers grow near the stem tips where leaves may differ in size and shape from those at base.

MARE'S TAIL (water milfoil family), found in central N.A., grows partially submersed or on marshy land. Short leaves, in whorls of 6 to 12, are rigid when emergent, limp when submersed. Spreads from rootstock.

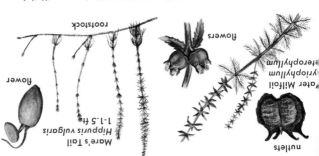

Mare's Tail
Hippuris vulgaris 1-1.5 ft.

flower

rootstock

Water Milfoil
Myriophyllum heterophyllum

flowers

nutlets

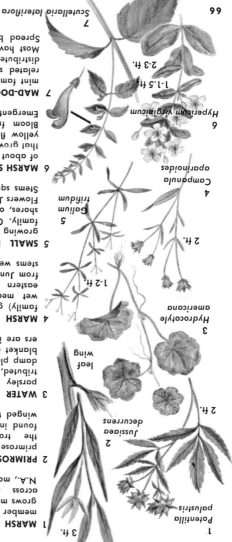

1 MARSH CINQUEFOIL is the only member of the rose family that grows mainly in wetlands. Found across central and northern N.A., mostly in bogs.

Potentilla palustris

2 PRIMROSE WILLOWS (evening primrose family) grow mostly in the tropics. Several species found in southern states. Leaves winged to stem.

Jussiaea decurrens

3 WATER PENNYWORT, in the parsley family, is widely distributed, growing in water or in damp places. Often forms dense blanket along shores. Tiny flowers are in axils of round leaves.

leaf wing

Hydrocotyle americana

4 MARSH BELLFLOWER (bluebell family) grows on shores and in wet meadows in central and eastern N.A. Flowers bloom from June to August. Submersed stems weak; leaves short.

Campanula aparinoides

5 SMALL BEDSTRAW is a low-growing herb of the madder family. Often forms mats along shores, occurring widely in N.A. Flowers June through September. Stems square, leaves whorled.

Galium trifidum

6 MARSH ST. JOHN'S-WORT is one of about 15 N.A. St. John's-worts that grow in wetlands. Most have yellow flowers; a few, purplish. Bloom from June to October. Emergent leaves may be dotted.

Hypericum virginicum

7 MAD-DOG SKULLCAP, of the mint family, is one of six closely related species that are widely distributed in wetlands in N.A. Most have purplish-blue flowers. Spread by underwater stems.

Scutellaria lateriflora

1 **SWAMPCANDLE LOOSESTRIFE** (primrose family) is a native of eastern N.A. Introduced in central and western states. Leaves opposite but appear whorled.

2 **FALSE LOOSESTRIFE** (primrose-willow family) common in eastern N.A., forms floating tangles in ponds and on wet shores. Leaves opposite.

3 **WATER WILLOW,** or Swamp Loosestrife (loosestrife family), grows throughout eastern N.A. Leaves whorled, sessile. Ducks eat seeds. Muskrats feed on the thick, submersed stems.

4 **WATER STARWORT** is a small plant with slender stems and spatula-shaped leaves that form floating clusters. Found in shallow ponds and slow-moving streams throughout N.A.

5 **WATER MARIGOLD** (composite family) has bright yellow flowers. The submersed leaves are finely branched, the emergent leaves deeply notched. Grows in quiet waters of central N.A.

6 **WATER PARSNIP** (parsley family) grows in ponds, lakes, and marshes throughout N.A. except in Southwest. White flowers in umbrella-shaped clusters. Fruits have corky ribs.

7 **HEDGE HYSSOP** (figwort family) grows in wet areas and temporary pools over most of N.A. The flowers are white, yellow, or bluish. The leaves are opposite and lack stems.

1
Lysimachia terrestris
2-8 ft.

2
Ludwigia palustris
2 ft.

3
Decodon verticillatus
1 ft.

4
Callitriche heterophylla
4-6 in.
1 ft.

5
Bidens beckii
6 ft.
fruit

6
Sium suave

7
Gratiola neglecta
1 ft.

WOODY PLANTS (trees, shrubs, and vines) of many species grow along shores and in wetlands. None is truly aquatic, but in a few groups nearly all species are found only in wet or moist soils. Most notable among these are the willows. Other groups, such as pines, oaks, birches, hawthorns, elms, and maples, include one to several species that commonly grow in wet places. All of these woody plants contribute to the total community. Only a few of the many possible examples are shown here.

WILLOWS (more than 100 species in N.A.) range from small shrubs to large trees, all but a few species growing in wet soils. All willows have narrow, pointed, alternate leaves. The male and female flowers (catkins) are borne on separate plants. Black Willow, either a shrub or a large tree, is found along shores, sometimes even standing in shallow waters, from eastern Canada to the Dakotas southward to the Gulf of Mexico.

POPLARS and aspens, which also belong to the willow family, have broad, heart-shaped leaves and catkins more drooping than those of willows. Like willows, their tiny seeds are plumed and wind-blown. Most poplars and aspens grow in dry soils, but a few are common along shores and in wetlands. These include the Swamp Cottonwood of western N.A. and the Eastern and Balsam cottonwoods of central and eastern N.A.

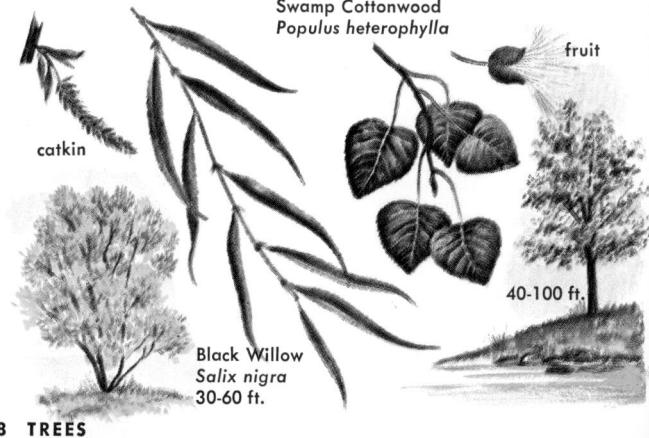

Swamp Cottonwood
Populus heterophylla

fruit

catkin

Black Willow
Salix nigra
30-60 ft.

40-100 ft.

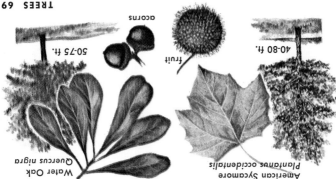

Water Oak
Quercus nigra

acorns

50-75 ft.

American Sycamore
Platanus occidentalis

fruit

40-80 ft.

OAKS (about 50 N.A. species) are mainly upland trees; a few grow in moist to wet soils. All produce acorns; leaves heavy, alternate, and of varied shapes. Water Oak is common in Southeast. Others are Overcup, Swamp, White, and Willow.

SYCAMORES grow in moist bottomlands and along shores. American Sycamore is widespread in the East; two other N.A. species grow in the Southwest. Seeds develop in dense, ball-shaped clusters; bark scales off or peels in shaggy plates.

TUPELOS grow in both wet and dry soils, but Water Tupelo (Sour Gum) is typical of coastal swamps and wetlands in the Southeast. The base of its trunk is often swollen. Black Gum, a more northern tree, is smaller and less common in wetlands.

CYPRESS trees are deciduous conebearers that grow in swamps and wetlands of the Southeast and lower Mississippi Valley. Note root extensions, or "knees," and swollen base of Bald Cypress trunk. Pond Cypress is smaller with scalelike leaves.

Water Tupelo
Nyssa aquatica

fruit

100 ft.

Bald Cypress
Taxodium distichum

cones

30-100 ft.

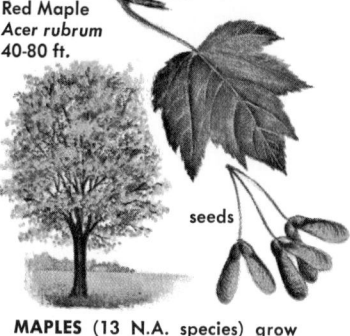

Red Maple
Acer rubrum
40-80 ft.

seeds

Green Ash
*Fraxinus
pennsylvanicus*
25-40 ft.

ASHES grow mainly in the moist bottomlands and along shores in the East. All of the some 20 N.A. species have opposite, compound leaves, thick twigs, and single-winged seeds. Most widely distributed in wetlands are Green Ash and Black Ash.

MAPLES (13 N.A. species) grow on dry slopes and also in moist bottomlands. Two eastern species —Red and Silver—are characteristic of wetlands; both are called Swamp Maple. Maples have simple, palmately lobed leaves. Their seeds have two wings.

BIRCHES total about 15 species in N.A., mainly in cool regions. Two are common in wetlands: Red, (River) Birch, found as far south as Florida and Texas; and the shrubby Western Birch of the Rockies. Birch bark is shaggy and peels off in strips. Hornbeam, or Blue Beech, also in

birch family, is a small tree with a sinewy trunk and blue-gray bark; grows along streams and in moist soils. Alders (10 N.A. birch family species, mainly western) commonly form dense thickets. Speckled Alder is an eastern wetland species; Red Alder, western.

River Birch
Betula nigra

Red Alder
Alnus rubra

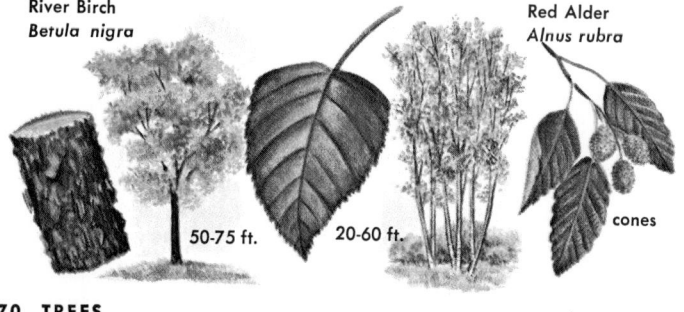

50-75 ft.

20-60 ft.

cones

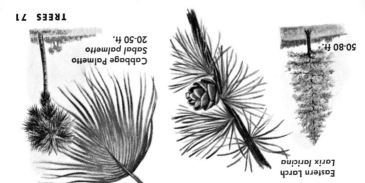

Cabbage Palmetto
Sabal palmetto 20-50 ft.

Eastern Larch
Larix laricina
50-80 ft.

CABBAGE PALMETTO, or Sabal Palmetto, is a member of the palm family. It often grows in wetlands from North Carolina southward and along Gulf Coast. Other, usually smaller, palmettos grow in southern pinelands.

TAMARACKS, or larches, are deciduous conifers (like cypress, p. 69). Cones stand upright. Most larches grow in dry soils, but Eastern Larch grows in swamps and along shores in central and eastern N.A. It is a pioneer in pond succession (p. 24).

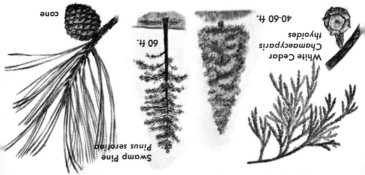

White Cedar
Chamaecyparis thyoides
40-60 ft.

Swamp Pine
Pinus serotina

cone

60 ft.

WHITE CEDAR is a strong-scented evergreen with scalelike leaves and small, fleshy cones. Grows most abundantly in brown-water swamps of South but north to Maine. Two species of arborvitae (*Thuja*), also called white cedars, grow in North.

SWAMP PINE grows along ponds and in swamps from New Jersey southward. Its needles are in bundles of 3, and the cones are round. Resembles Pitch Pine, which like most pines (more than 30 N.A. species), grows best in dry soil.

SWEET GALE (waxmyrtle family) grows in wetlands of northern and central N.A. Its twigs give off a spicy odor when bruised. Flowers are catkins, the male and female on separate plants.

BOG ROSEMARY (heath family) is a low, rather inconspicuous shrub that grows in bogs and ponds in middle N.A. Spreads from rootstock. Grows to about 2 feet tall.

BUTTONBUSH (madder family) bears small globular masses of flowers at ends of leafless stalks. Usually a shrub but may reach height of 50 feet. Seeds are eaten by waterfowl.

SWAMP SUMAC, or Poison Sumac, forms thickets. Other sumacs (about 12 N.A. species) grow in dry soils. Like Poison Ivy, also in cashew family, it has poisonous sap. Leaves pinnate, alternate; turn red. Flowers produced greenish fruit clusters.

LEATHERLEAF (heath family) grows in bogs and along pond margins in central N.A. The drooping flower clusters are attractive as are the purplish leaves in winter.

RED OSIER DOGWOOD (dogwood family) grows in wet thickets throughout middle N.A. A low-growing shrub easily recognized in winter when red bark of new growth shows against snow. Flowers in May. Berry-like fruits are wildlife food.

SWAMP ROSE, with erect and stiff stems, grows nearly 8 feet tall. Its flowers are not very showy. Grows throughout central and eastern N.A.

COMMON WINTERBERRY, one of about 15 N.A. holly family trees in eastern N.A., has alternate, deciduous leaves. Red fruits a winter wildlife food.

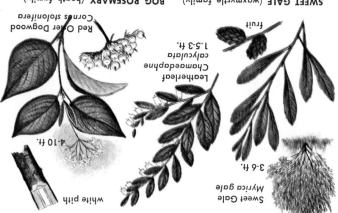

Red Osier Dogwood
Cornus stolonifera

white pith

4-10 ft.

Leatherleaf
Chamaedaphne
calyculata 1.5-3 ft.

fruit

Sweet Gale
Myrica gale

3-6 ft.

Greenbrier
Smilax hispida

Fox Grape
Vitis labrusca

Limber Honeysuckle
Lonicera dioica

WOODY VINES may form impenetrable tangles in shore and wetland thickets. Greenbriers (*Smilax*), grape (*Vitis*), and honeysuckle (*Lonicera*) are widespread groups. Each consists of about two dozen species, including one to several typical of wet soils. Greenbriers (holly family) have stout, usually straight spines on green stems. Greenbriers and grapes climb by means of tendrils—in greenbriers, arising in pairs; in grapes, branched at tip. Honeysuckle, sometimes shrubby, has hollow branches.

Swamp Sumac
Rhus vernix
5-20 ft.
fruit

Common Winterberry
Ilex verticillata
5-15 ft.

Buttonbush
Cephalanthus occidentalis

Swamp Rose
Rosa palustris
fruit

Bog Rosemary
Andromeda glaucophylla
fruit

ANIMALS

Animals representing nearly all of the major groups, or phyla, are found in fresh waters. They range in size from microscopic one-celled animals (protozoans) to large many-celled animals (metazoans), such as worms, insects, fishes, and alligators. Some spend their entire life in water, hence are wholly aquatic. Others are aquatic only in some of their life stages. Many land dwellers feed and rear their young in marshes or along the shores of ponds, lakes, and streams.

Animals that live in ponds and lakes have the same needs as those that live on land. There must be food available, some degree of protection from predators, and an opportunity to reproduce. The chemical material of animals' bodies may be passed from one animal to another as prey is eaten by predator, but eventually it is returned to the pond cycle when the animals die and their bodies decompose (pp. 22-23).

MAJOR GROUPS OF POND ANIMALS

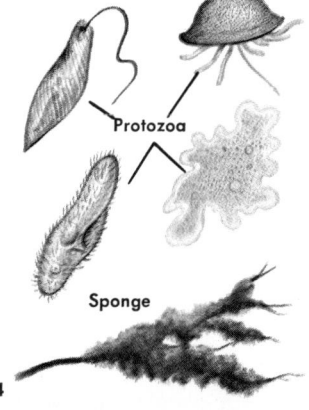

Protozoa

Sponge

ONE-CELLED ANIMALS, or Protozoa, are the simplest of all animals. They are abundant in pond and lake waters, especially in those enriched with organic matter. With simple plants (algae, p. 31), these tiny animals form the plankton pastures that are the basic link in food chains.   Page 76.

SPONGES are mostly marine, the members of only one family living in fresh water. The larvae are free-swimming, but the adults are attached, sometimes forming spreading encrustations on twigs or rocks.   Page 77.

HYDRAS (Coelenterata) have a saclike body of two layers of cells and a fringe of tentacles around body opening. Page 78.

ROTIFERS, found only in fresh waters, are commonly mistaken for one-celled animals. Wheel-like rotation of cilia draws in food and water.   Page 80.

MOSS ANIMALS, or Bryozoans, are mainly marine. Few species live in fresh water, growing in "mossy" colonies.   Page 81.

WORMS are never conspicuous but they may be abundant under stones or in debris. The segmented worms (pp. 82-83) include aquatic, bloodsucking leeches and also earthworms. Most flatworms (p. 84) are parasites; a few are free-living. Smaller groups on pp. 118-119.

ARTHROPODS are the most numerous of all animals. Crayfish, insects, and spiders are the large conspicuous types. Others are minute but equally important as food for fishes and other animals.   Page 85.

MOLLUSKS have a soft body enclosed in a limy shell—a single, coiled structure (as in snails) or two hinged valves (as in clams).   Page 114.

VERTEBRATES are the fishes, amphibians, reptiles, birds, mammals—all have backbones. Some are plant eaters; others are carnivorous, in the top position in most food chains.   Page 120.

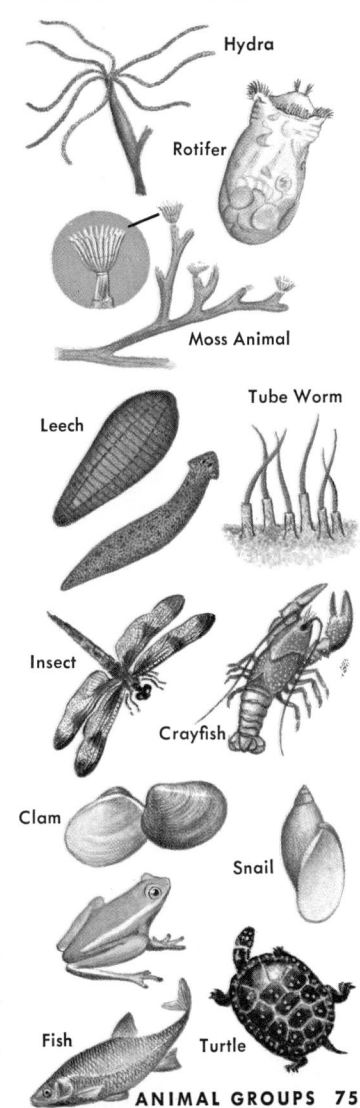

Hydra

Rotifer

Moss Animal

Tube Worm

Leech

Insect

Crayfish

Clam

Snail

Fish

Turtle

ONE-CELLED ANIMALS (Protozoa) are microscopic or nearly so, yet in their single cell they carry on all life processes: reproduction, excretion, digestion, respiration, and irritability. Protozoans occur in a great variety of body forms and have many different methods of movement. The more than 30,000 species live in a wide range of moist and aquatic habitats. In numbers, they probably exceed all other animals in ponds and lakes. Protozoans reproduce by budding of a new individual from the parent, by splitting of the parent cell to form two new cells, and by fusion of cells or cell parts.

Some protozoans feed on algae, yeasts, bacteria, and other protozoans. Others subsist on dissolved or decaying substances, and a few manufacture foods. In turn, they are preyed upon by hydras (p. 78), rotifers (p. 80), and small crustaceans (p. 86).

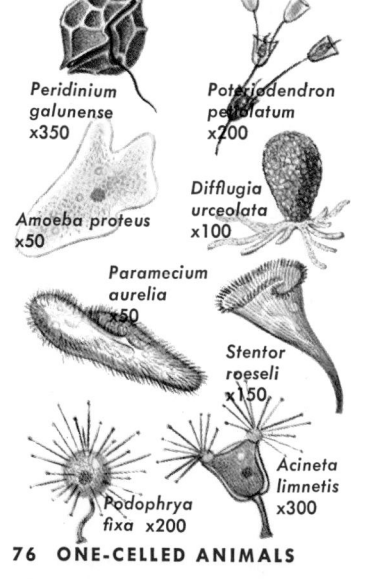

Peridinium galunense x350

Poteriodendron petiolatum x200

Amoeba proteus x50

Difflugia urceolata x100

Paramecium aurelia x50

Stentor roeseli x150

Podophrya fixa x200

Acineta limnetis x300

MASTIGOPHORA have whiplike extensions of protoplasm (flagella). Many are free-swimming single cells; others form colonies. Often classed as plants (p. 36).

SARCODINA move by flowing cell extensions called pseudopodia. Some secrete shells; others are naked.

CILIATA have numerous hairlike projections of protoplasm (cilia) that beat in unison. They propel the animal and create currents that bring food to the cell. Some are free-swimming, others live attached to objects.

SUCTORIA are mostly parasites: some cause disease. Free-living suctorians have suckerlike "arms" for grasping food and are attached by stalks.

SPONGES (Porifera) are simple colonial animals grow-ing attached and submerged. Sponges are mainly marine. Fresh-water sponges, all members of one family of about 150 species, live in the clear shallow waters of ponds and lakes. Though usually dull creamy or brownish, some sponge colonies are green due to algae living in them. They range in size from an inch or less to massive encrustations covering many square yards.

Sponges feed on floating or swimming microscopic animals and plants that are trapped in their pores as water circulates through. A sponge's body is strength-end by rodlike spicules that, in all fresh-water forms, are composed of silica. In autumn some sponges form gem-mules, small rounded structures that drop to the bottom when the colony dies in cold weather. The following spring each gemmule develops into a new sponge.

SPONGILLA of many species are widely distributed in streams and standing waters. They commonly occur in association with a spe-cies of Meyenia.

MEYENIA species are wide-spread and tolerate slight pollu-tion. Some live only in acid waters, others in alkaline. Small animals live inside the sponges.

Spongilla
lacustris

gemmules on
dying sponge

gemmule

Meyenia
mülleri

gemmule

Spicules of fresh-water sponges are composed almost wholly of silica.

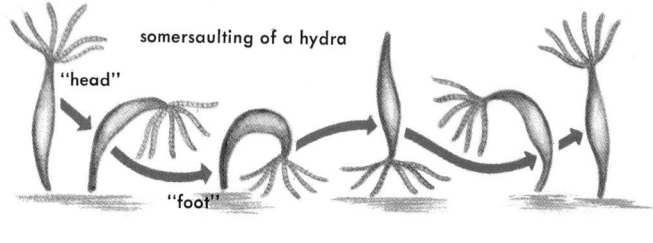
somersaulting of a hydra

"head"

"foot"

HYDRAS (Coelenterata) have a saclike body consisting of only two layers of cells. A single opening rimmed with tentacles serves both for taking in food and for eliminating wastes. Most coelenterates—the sea anemones, corals, and jellyfishes—are marine.

Hydras, usually less than 1 inch long, live in unpolluted pond or lake waters. Their food consists of one-celled animals, small crustaceans, worms, insects, and other tiny animals. They capture them by special "cells" (nematocysts) in the tentacles that surround the body opening. Some nematocysts entangle or stick to the food organisms; others sting the prey, paralyzing it.

Hydras can move by inching along slowly on their "foot" or may turn end over end in a somersaulting movement. They reproduce either sexually or by forming buds that break off and grow into new animals.

nematocysts

sticky

entangling

bud

BROWN HYDRA is slimmest toward its "foot." Its tentacles are three or four times the length of its body. Widely distributed in cool ponds and lakes in N.A.

Hydra oligactis

tentacles

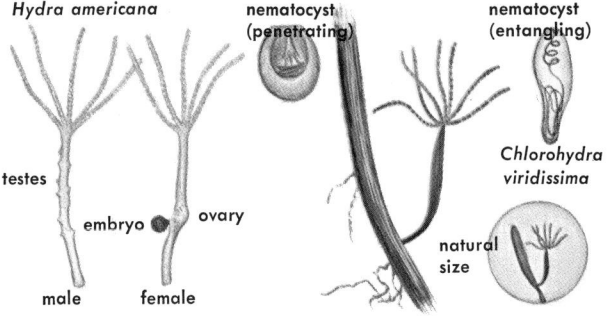

Hydra americana

testes

embryo   ovary

male   female

nematocyst (penetrating)

nematocyst (entangling)

Chlorohydra viridissima

natural size

AMERICAN HYDRA is white or grayish and is not stalked. Its tentacles are shorter than the body. Common throughout eastern N.A., it lives in standing waters and in sluggish streams. It attaches itself to submerged objects by its base.

GREEN HYDRA is grass-green due to algae living in cells lining its body. Some of these are passed from parent to offspring with the egg. Green Hydra gets some nutrition from the algae but also feeds on organic debris. Common in N.A.

FRESH-WATER JELLYFISH. The single species known in N.A. is generally similar to its marine relatives. Usually no more than 0.5 inch in diameter, it appears sporadically in lakes, ponds, and even in aquariums. Its life cycle includes a small attached polyp stage, when it is similar in appearance to hydras.

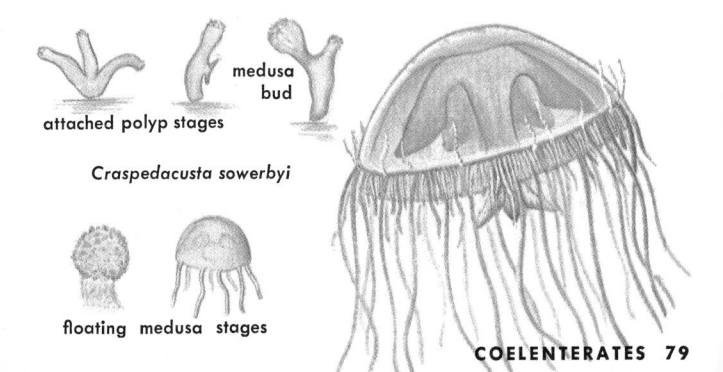

medusa bud

attached polyp stages

Craspedacusta sowerbyi

floating medusa stages

ROTIFERS (wheel animalcules) are found in all types of quiet waters. Rotifers are tiny, many of them microscopic and sometimes mistaken for one-celled animals. Their name refers to the rotating movement of the hairlike projections (cilia) on the front of the body. At the rear is a base, or foot, that secretes a "glue" by which the rotifer attaches to objects. The 1,700 known species are widely distributed. Some live in the shore zone; others are part of the floating plankton. Some feed on algae; others pierce plant stems and suck out the juices. Many are predaceous. Rotifers, in turn, are the food of worms and crustaceans. Some rotifers secrete a gelatinous covering and remain dormant for months if the pool in which they are living dries up.

OPEN-WATER ROTIFERS include *Keratella, Polyarthra,* and *Asplanchna.* In the shore zone are sessile (attached) rotifers, such as *Floscularia,* and others, such as *Philodina,* that crawl about on the bottom or in dense mats of plants. Water chemistry also determines the distribution of some species. *Brachionus* is found mostly in alkaline ponds of the western states. *Monostyla* is most common in acid waters. Rotifers can be captured by straining pond water through a plankton net. (p. 28).

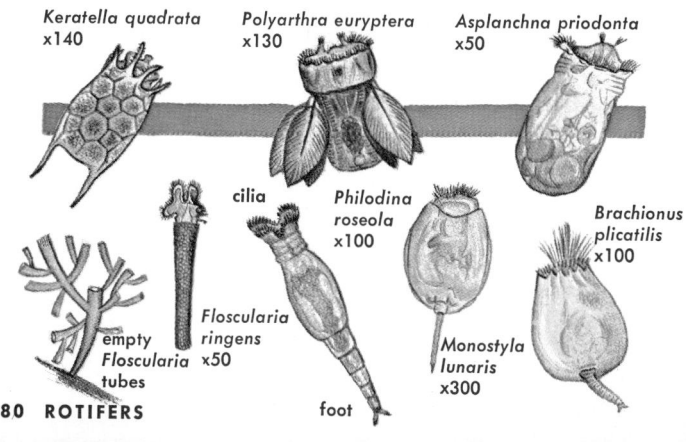

Keratella quadrata
x140

Polyarthra euryptera
x130

Asplanchna priodonta
x50

cilia

Philodina roseola
x100

Brachionus plicatilis
x100

empty *Floscularia* tubes

Floscularia ringens
x50

Monostyla lunaris
x300

foot

MOSS ANIMALS (Bryozoa) grow in encrusting colonies on submerged objects. Large colonies may contain thousands of individuals (zooids), best seen when magnified. When feeding, their waving tentacles create currents that bring algae, protozoans, and decayed matter to the animals. If disturbed, tentacles are retracted.

A colony grows by budding, but sexual reproduction also occurs, usually in summer. Some species produce thick-walled buds (statoblasts) that resist cold or drought. When conditions are favorable, these germinate and become new colonies. Buds equipped with hooks may be carried on other aquatic animals from one location to another. Fewer than 50 of the more than 3,500 species live in fresh water. About 15 occur in N.A.

COLONIES of bryozoans are common in still waters, rare in polluted waters. *Fredericella* usually inhabits shallow rocky bottoms but has been found in water more than 600 feet deep. *Plumatella* lives in ponds and sluggish streams. *Pectinatella* is unable to tolerate low temperatures and dies in water colder than about 60° F. Large gelatinous masses of *Pectinatella* may clog intake pipes in waterwork. *Plumatella* and *Fredericella* are found the world over; *Pectinatella* only in N.A.

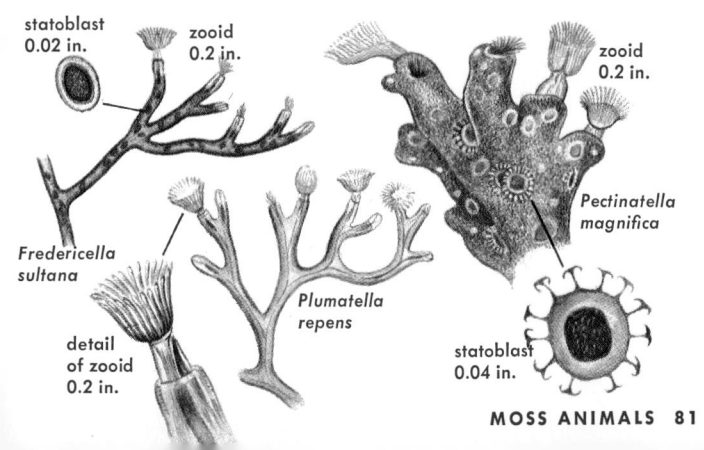

statoblast
0.02 in.

zooid
0.2 in.

zooid
0.2 in.

Fredericella sultana

Pectinatella magnifica

detail of zooid
0.2 in.

Plumatella repens

statoblast
0.04 in.

WORMS are animals belonging to several major unrelated groups that share a generally similar shape These include the flatworms (p. 84) and also smaller groups (pp. 118-119). Segmented worms (Annelida) are the earthworms, mainly land dwellers; leeches, found primarily in fresh water; and sandworms, mainly marine.

A few species of the earthworm group live in freshwater ponds and lakes. Some are abundant in decaying vegetation or in floating masses of algae. Others feed on organic matter as they burrow in the bottom mud.

EARTHWORM GROUP (OLIGOCHAETA)

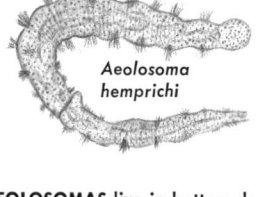

Aeolosoma hemprichi

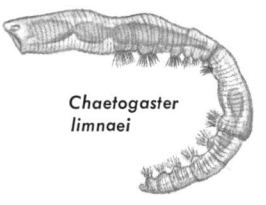

Chaetogaster limnaei

AEOLOSOMAS live in bottom debris or in plant growths. Some species swim. Most species have red, yellow, or other pigment spots. Length to about 0.5 inch.

CHAETOGASTERS feed on small crustaceans and insect larvae. Their mouths are large. Chaetogasters are generally colorless. Length, 0.5 inch.

DEROS are tube builders common in debris or on floating leaves. From 0.3 to 0.5 inch long. Bristly body ends in finger-like projections.

TUBIFEX worms are reddish bottom-dwelling tube builders. The head is buried in the mud, and the tail waves above. Length about 1 inch.

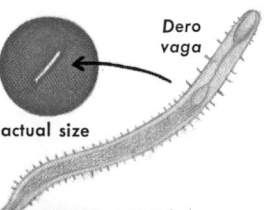

Dero vaga

actual size

Tubifex tubifex

Leeches are flattened, segmented worms, often abundant in calm, shallow, warm waters in which the bottom is cluttered with debris. They are seldom found in acid waters, and they survive the drying up of ponds by burrowing into the bottom mud. Leeches shun light. They move by "looping"—alternately attaching the mouth sucker and tail sucker to the surface. Some kinds are graceful swimmers. Bloodsucking leeches have well-developed jaws, in contrast to those of scavenger and carnivorous species.

LEECHES (HIRUDINEA)

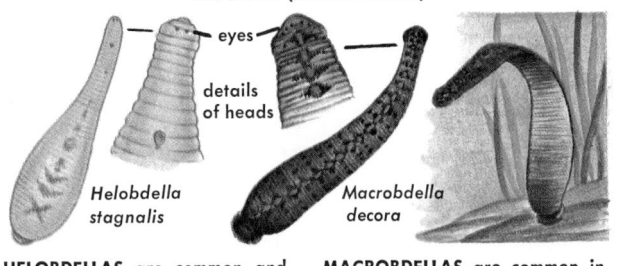

eyes

details
of heads

*Helobdella
stagnalis*

*Macrobdella
decora*

HELOBDELLAS are common and widely distributed in temperate waters. Species shown is a parasite of snails; others of fish, frogs, and turtles. To 3 inches.

MACROBDELLAS are common in the northern U.S. and southern Canada. Feed only on blood of vertebrates. To 10 inches long, with red and black spots.

ERPOBDELLAS feed on invertebrates, fish, and frogs; occasionally attack humans. Widely distributed. They reach a length of about 4 inches.

HAEMOPSIS leeches often travel considerable distances from water. Feed on living or dead invertebrates. Giant Haemopsis may stretch to 18 inches long.

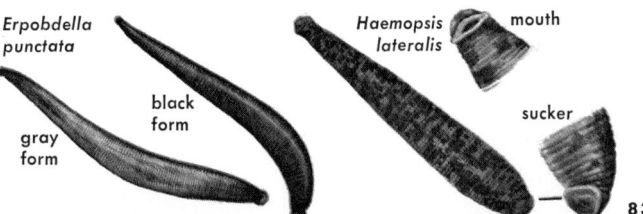

*Erpobdella
punctata*

black
form

gray
form

*Haemopsis
lateralis*

mouth

sucker

FLATWORMS (Platyhelminthes), such as flukes and tapeworms, are parasites. Turbellarians are free-living flatworms.

Turbellarians avoid light. During the day they remain on the underside of stones, leaves, or other submerged objects. Their mouth, the only opening to the digestive tract, is at the end of an extendible tube about midway on the underside. They have light-sensitive eyespots in the head region. Turbellarians eat small animals, living or dead. They glide along rocks or sticks by using the hairlike cilia on their undersurface. When turbellarians reproduce sexually, the fertilized eggs are usually encased in shell-like cocoons. In asexual reproduction a crosswise division of the body forms two parts, each becoming a complete animal.

DUGESIAS are widespread in N.A. *D. tigrina* may be blotched with black or brown or have a light streak lengthwise down its body. It has blunt, rounded ear lobes (auricles). *D. doratocephala,* with pointed ear lobes, is 1 inch or more long, the largest free-living flatworm in N.A. Common in spring-fed marshes.

CATENULAS are small (less than 0.5 inch), slender, usually whitish worms of stagnant waters. The body consists of many separate units in a chain.

PROCOTYLAS, common in eastern N.A., have tiny eyes (2-7) and a large sucking organ used in feeding.

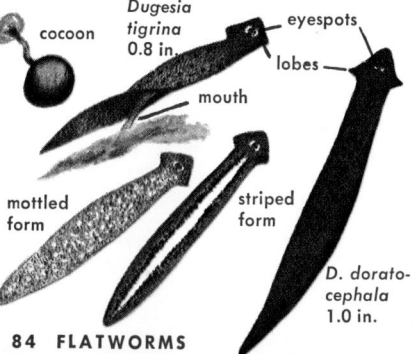

cocoon

Dugesia tigrina 0.8 in.

eyespots

lobes

mouth

mottled form

striped form

D. doratocephala 1.0 in.

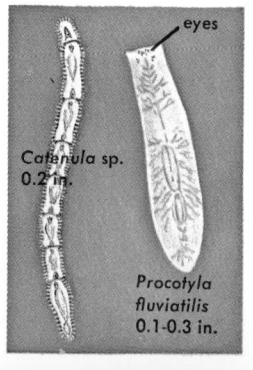

eyes

Catenula sp. 0.2 in.

Procotyla fluviatilis 0.1-0.3 in.

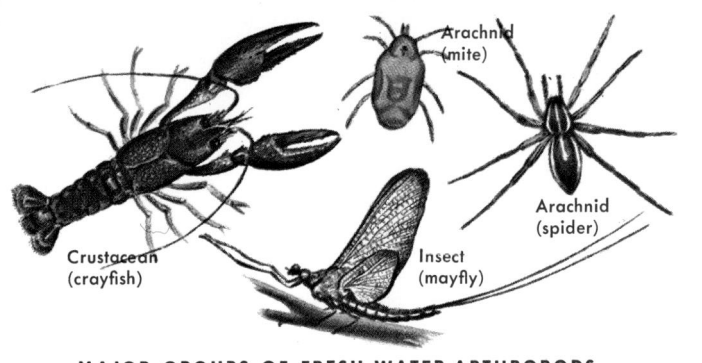

MAJOR GROUPS OF FRESH-WATER ARTHROPODS

ARTHROPODS, or Joint-legged Animals, have a segmented external skeleton and well-developed circulatory, digestive, reproductive, and nervous systems. Many exhibit complex behavior. Arthropods in three classes are abundant in ponds and lakes.

The crustaceans (Crustacea) typically have two body divisions—cephalothorax (head-thorax) and abdomen. They have two pairs of antennae, one pair of appendages per body segment, and gills. Included in the group are shrimplike animals, crayfish, and also numerous minute forms (p. 86).

Insects (Insecta) usually have three body divisions—head, thorax, and abdomen. They have only one pair of antennae and three pairs of appendages, plus wings attached to the thorax. Respiration is through tracheae. Included are mayflies, dragonflies, beetles, bugs, flies, and others (p. 94).

Spiders and mites (Arachnida) have two body divisions—cephalothorax and abdomen. They have no antennae, four pairs of appendages, and either tracheae or book lungs. Those few that live underwater must come to the surface to breathe (p. 113).

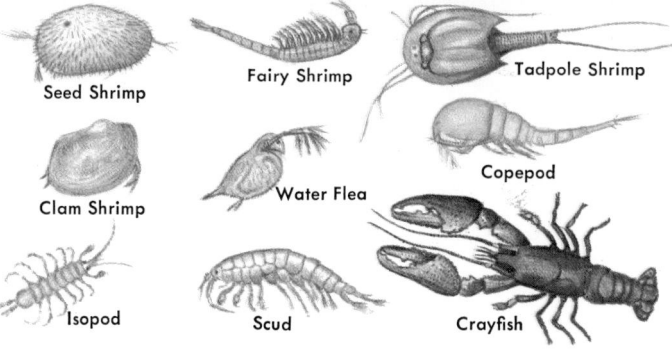

Seed Shrimp

Fairy Shrimp

Tadpole Shrimp

Clam Shrimp

Water Flea

Copepod

Isopod

Scud

Crayfish

CRUSTACEANS are nearly all aquatic, and most of the about 30,000 species are marine. They are largely scavengers or feed on plants, but some are predators, others parasites. Listed below are the groups that occur in or near fresh water.

SEED SHRIMPS (Ostracoda): flat body in bivalved carapace; 2 (sometimes 3) pairs of rounded appendages on thorax. No growth lines on shell. Page 87.

FAIRY SHRIMPS (Anostraca): no carapace; eyes stalked; 11 to 17 pairs of leaflike appendages, used for swimming and respiration. Pages 88-89.

TADPOLE SHRIMPS (Notostraca): shieldlike carapace over part of abdomen; eyes not stalked; 40 to 60 pairs of appendages. Pages 88-89.

CLAM SHRIMPS (Conchostraca): bivalved carapace with lines of growth (as in clams); eyes not stalked; 10 to 28 pairs of flat appendages. Pages 88-89.

WATER FLEAS (Cladocera): all of body except head in carapace; 4 to 6 pairs of flat appendages. Pages 88-89

COPEPODS (Copepoda): cylindrical body; 5 or 6 pairs of rounded appendages. Page 90.

ISOPODS (Isopoda): body flattened top to bottom; no carapace. Page 91.

SCUDS (Amphipoda): slightly compressed; no carapace; hop when out of water. Page 91.

CRAYFISH AND SHRIMPS (Decapoda): body nearly rounded; distinct cephalothorax enclosed in carapace; specialized appendages for feeding, walking, swimming, reproduction Page 92.

SEED SHRIMPS (Ostracoda), usually less than 0.1 inch long, are bivalved (clamlike) crustaceans found in fresh waters of all types. They are especially common in mats of algae or other vegetation and also in mud on pond bottoms. Many of the some 150 N.A. species are brightly colored. Some have dark patterns on their valves. Their two pairs of antennae are protruded from between the shells when opened and, with other appendages, aid in swimming. Eggs are laid on plant stems and in debris. The males of many species are unknown; the females lay unfertilized eggs that develop into larvae. A larva, or nauplius, is quite different from the adult and goes through several stages before reaching maturity. Seed shrimps are scavengers. They are eaten by small fishes. Three common pond species are shown below.

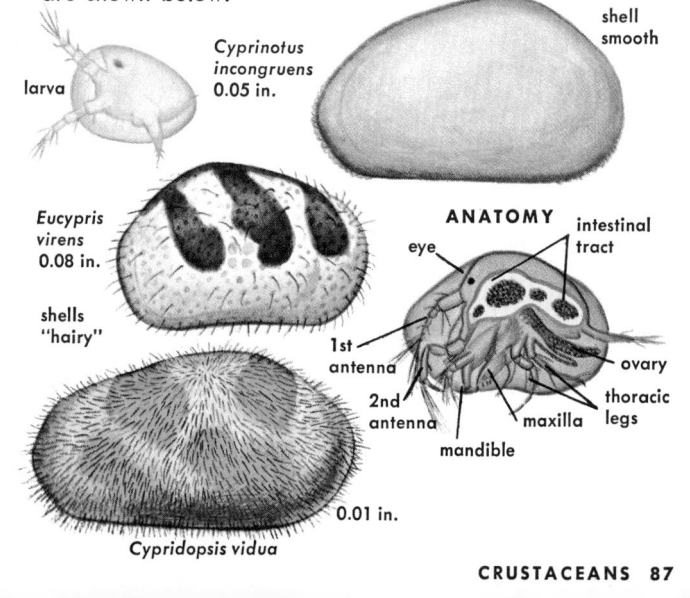

larva

Cyprinotus incongruens
0.05 in.

shell smooth

Eucypris virens
0.08 in.

shells "hairy"

ANATOMY

eye

1st antenna

2nd antenna

mandible

maxilla

intestinal tract

ovary

thoracic legs

0.01 in.

Cypridopsis vidua

FAIRY SHRIMPS (Anostraca) appear irregularly in small ponds or in temporary pools and often become very numerous. They are seldom more than 1 inch long. Fairy shrimps swim on their back. When mating, the male holds the female with claspers that develop from his second pair of antennae and from an outgrowth on the front of his head. The female has an egg sac behind her gill-legs. About 25 species, including the Brine Shrimp familiar to aquarists, are found in N.A. Two common species are illustrated on p. 89.

TADPOLE SHRIMPS (Notostraca) have 40 to 60 pairs of broad swimimng appendages beneath their carapace. They also crawl and burrow in the fine silt on the bottom. Length to about 1 inch.

CLAM SHRIMPS (Conchostraca) are common in warm shallow waters of ponds and lakes and may also appear in temporary pools. Bivalved shell is held shut by a strong muscle. Length less than 0.5 inch.

WATER FLEAS (Cladocera), abundant in all kinds of fresh water, swim jerkily by means of the enlarged second pair of antennae. Water fleas eat algae, microscopic animals, and organic debris swept into their mouth in current of water created by the waving of their legs. In turn, they are eaten in great numbers by small fishes. In some species the shape of the female's head changes seasonally.

CHYDORUS is a water flea occurring in plankton; *Daphnia* and *Bosmina,* both in open water and shore zones. *Scapholeberis* lives on the underside of the surface film, held there by special body bristles. *Leptodora,* a transparent carnivore, usually comes to surface only at night. This largest of the water fleas is common in the plankton of northern ponds and lakes.

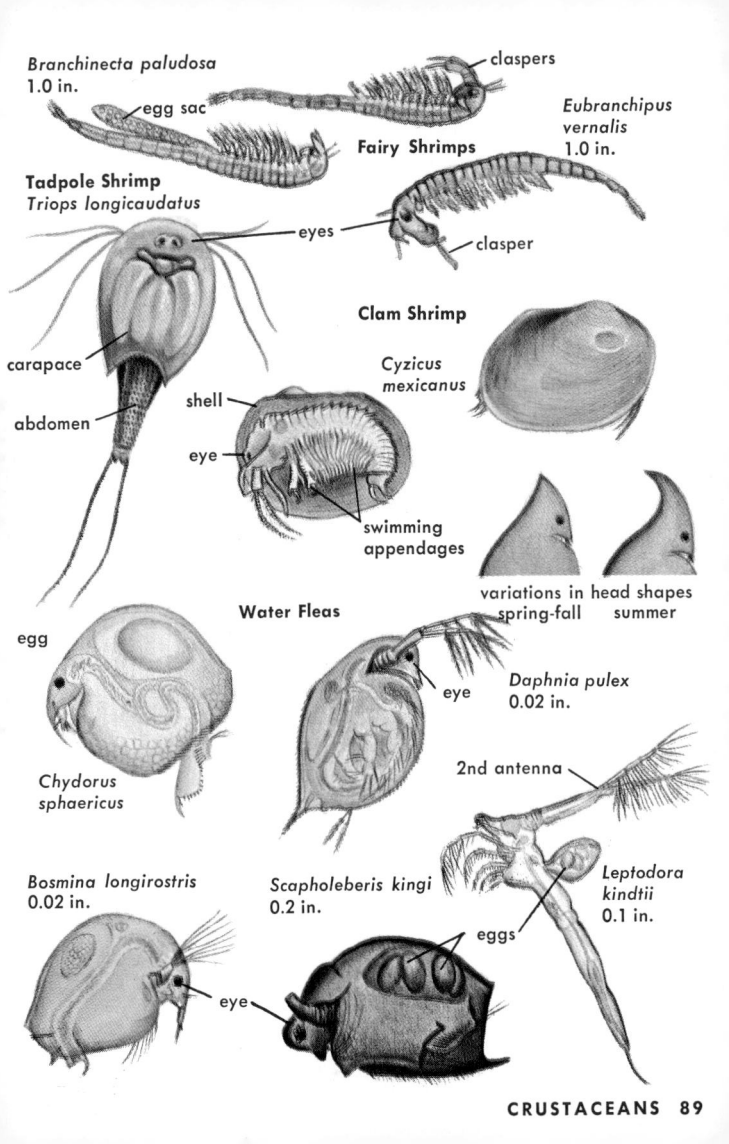

Branchinecta paludosa
1.0 in.

claspers

egg sac

Fairy Shrimps

Eubranchipus vernalis
1.0 in.

Tadpole Shrimp
Triops longicaudatus

eyes

clasper

carapace

abdomen

Clam Shrimp

Cyzicus mexicanus

shell

eye

swimming appendages

variations in head shapes
spring-fall   summer

Water Fleas

egg

Chydorus sphaericus

eye

Daphnia pulex
0.02 in.

2nd antenna

Bosmina longirostris
0.02 in.

Scapholeberis kingi
0.2 in.

eggs

Leptodora kindtii
0.1 in.

eye

COPEPODS (Copepoda) are small crustaceans (about 0.1 inch long) found everywhere in shallow waters and in open-water plankton of ponds and lakes. Some cling to vegetation and are found even in damp debris above the waterline. A few kinds, such as *Argulus,* are parasitic on fishes and other aquatic animals but seldom cause much harm. During the breeding season, one or two egg sacs develop on each female. The young pass through five or six nauplius stages before maturity. Copepods feed on algae, bacteria, and organic debris. They are food themselves for larger animals, though not as important as food for fishes as are water fleas (p. 88). There are three groups of free-living copepods.

Diaptomus oregonensis

0.08 in.

CALANOID COPEPODS have antennae nearly as long as their body. *Diaptomus* and others live in plankton and feed on filtered organic matter from water.

CYCLOPOID COPEPODS have antennae about as long as the broad "trunk region" of body. *Cyclops* and others live in open water. They seize and bite their small prey.

HARPACTICOID COPEPODS, with short antennae, live in silt and plant debris. *Moraria* (below) and others feed by scraping algae and detritus from rocks and other objects.

Cyclops bicuspidatus

0.08 in.

egg sacs

nauplius (larva) of Cyclops

Moraria duthiei

0.06

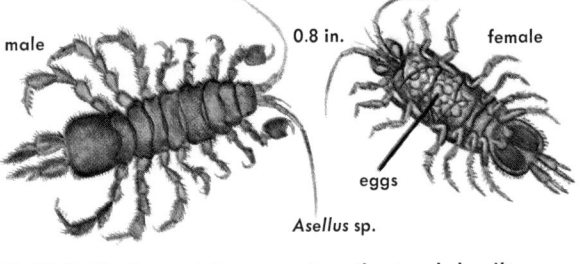

male   0.8 in.   female

eggs

Asellus sp.

ISOPODS (Isopoda) are primarily land-dwelling crustaceans (pill bugs, etc.). A few, such as *Asellus*, live in water. Usually less than an inch long, these flattened, dark-colored animals are mainly scavengers, living on decaying plants on the bottom.

SCUDS (Amphipoda), also called Side-swimmers, are widely distributed in ponds and are found even in the deep waters of large lakes. Flattened sidewise like fleas, scuds usually live close to the bottom or among submerged objects; they avoid light. Some, such as *Gammarus,* grow to about 0.5 inch long, but most scuds are much smaller. They are scavengers on plant and animal debris; and in turn, they are eaten by fishes that feed among plants or off the bottom. Scuds are the intermediate hosts for tapeworms and other parasites of frogs, fishes, and birds.

GAMMARUS resembles *Hyalella* but first antennae are as long as second and have a small branch. Mate spring through fall.

HYALELLA occurs abundantly in masses of waterweeds and algae. Its first antennae are shorter than the second.

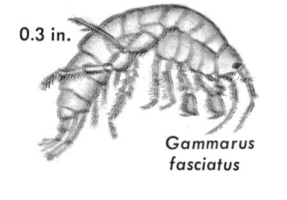

0.3 in.

Gammarus fasciatus

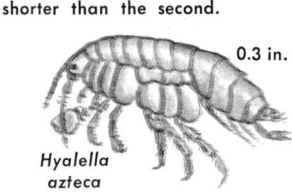

0.3 in.

Hyalella azteca

CRAYFISH AND FRESH-WATER SHRIMPS (Decapoda) are relatives of marine crabs, lobsters, and shrimps. They have a carapace over head and thorax and five pairs of walking legs, the first pair with large pincers used in holding and tearing food. More than 200 species of crayfish live in N.A. Some species are found only in ponds, others in streams, and still others in wetlands in burrows that can be identified by their above-ground "chimneys" made of mud balls from the digging.

Crayfish usually hide in burrows or under objects

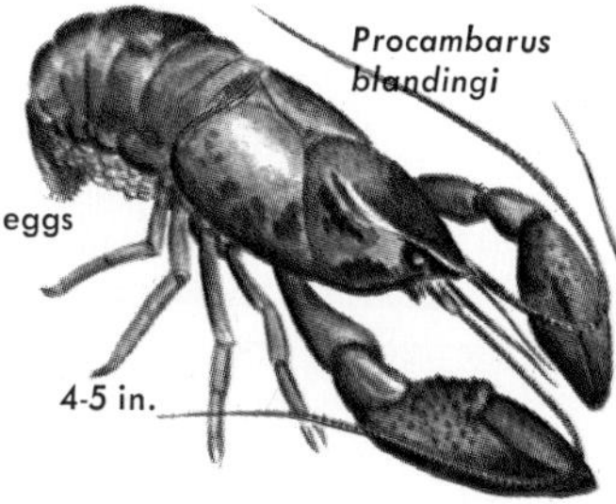

Procambarus blandingi

eggs

4-5 in.

POND CRAYFISH live in almost all kinds of fresh waters in central and southeastern N.A. During dry seasons, they burrow into wet soil.

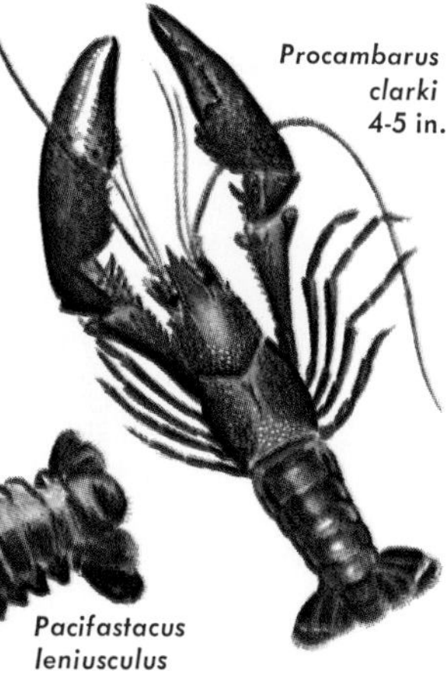

Procambarus clarki
4-5 in.

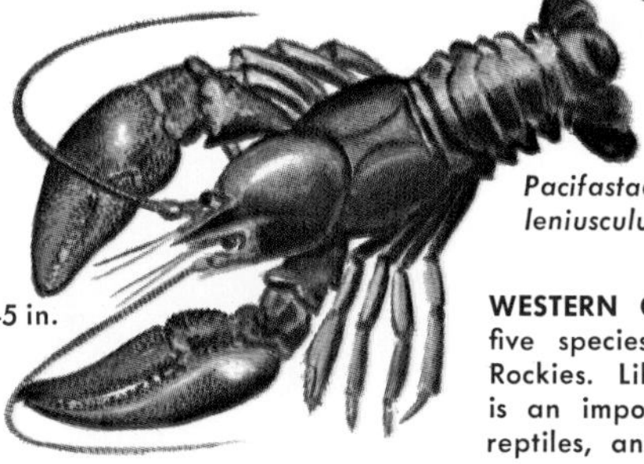

SWAMP CRAYFISH inhabit sluggish waters of southeastern N.A.; introduced to western states. In autumn males migrate overland in droves to new waters.

Pacifastacus leniusculus

4-5 in.

WESTERN CRAYFISH is one of five species in waters west of Rockies. Like other crayfish, it is an important food of fishes, reptiles, and other carnivores.

during the day. They are active at night. Their food consists mainly of plants, though they will eat animal food when available. The female carries the fertilized eggs attached to appendages (swimmerets) on her abdomen. Young crayfish pass through three stages (instars) before becoming adults. Crayfish shed, or molt, their hard exoskeleton as they grow.

Fresh-water shrimps, or prawns, live in plant growth in shallow water. They look like salt-water shrimps and are smaller than crayfish.

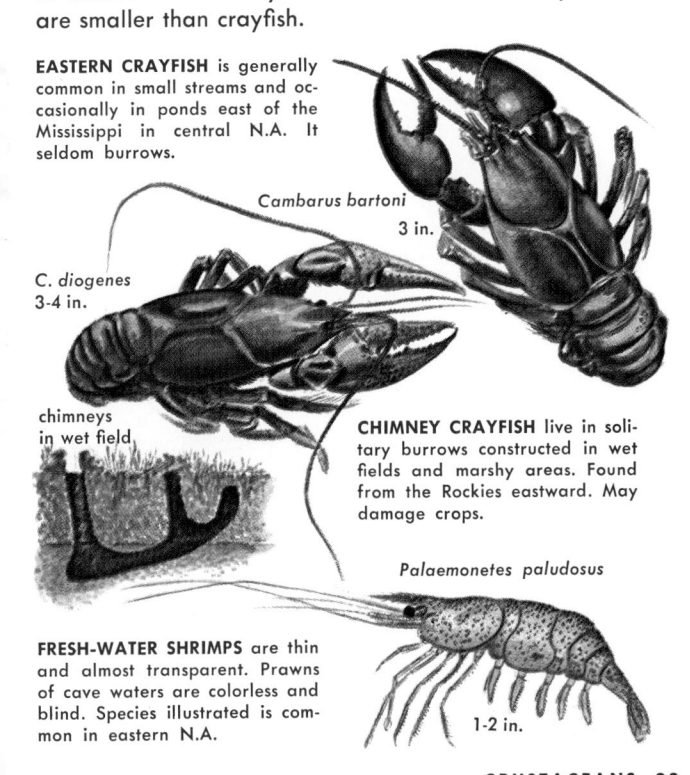

EASTERN CRAYFISH is generally common in small streams and occasionally in ponds east of the Mississippi in central N.A. It seldom burrows.

Cambarus bartoni
3 in.

C. diogenes
3-4 in.

chimneys in wet field

CHIMNEY CRAYFISH live in solitary burrows constructed in wet fields and marshy areas. Found from the Rockies eastward. May damage crops.

Palaemonetes paludosus

FRESH-WATER SHRIMPS are thin and almost transparent. Prawns of cave waters are colorless and blind. Species illustrated is common in eastern N.A.

1-2 in.

CRUSTACEANS 93

INSECTS (Insecta). About 5,000 species of insects in N.A. spend some or all of their life in water. Adult insects have three body regions: head, thorax, and abdomen. The thorax bears three pairs of jointed legs and, in most orders, two pairs of wings. Immature stages —nymphs, larvae, and pupae—are abundant and important in the food webs of ponds and lakes.

ORDERS OF AQUATIC INSECTS

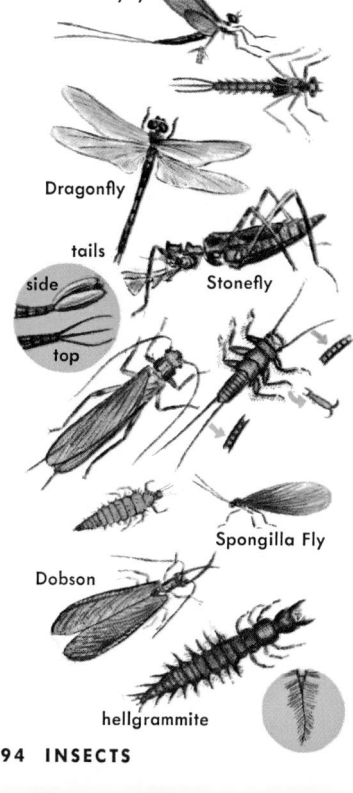

Mayfly

Dragonfly

tails

side

top

Stonefly

Spongilla Fly

Dobson

hellgrammite

MAYFLIES (Ephemeroptera): the aquatic nymphs, or naiads, swim actively. Two or three long, feathery tail appendages; flaplike gills along abdomen; one claw on each foot.   Page 96.

DRAGONFLIES AND DAMSELFLIES (Odonata): nymphs, or naiads, are active. Damselfly nymphs have three leaflike structures extending from tail; dragonfly nymphs do not. In both, masklike scoop covers chewing mouthparts.   Pages 98-99.

STONEFLIES (Plecoptera): nymphs have two, jointed tail appendages; two claws on each foot.   Page 100.

SPONGILLA FLIES (Neuroptera): small, active larvae have many bristles over body. Feed in freshwater sponges. Page 100.

ALDERFLIES, DOBSONS, AND FISHFLIES (Megaloptera): predatory larvae with stout appendages; single tail filament (alderflies) or pair (hellgrammites).   Page 100.

SPRINGTAILS (Collembola): less than 0.2 inch long; forked appendage on underside used for springing on water surface or on shore. Page 100.

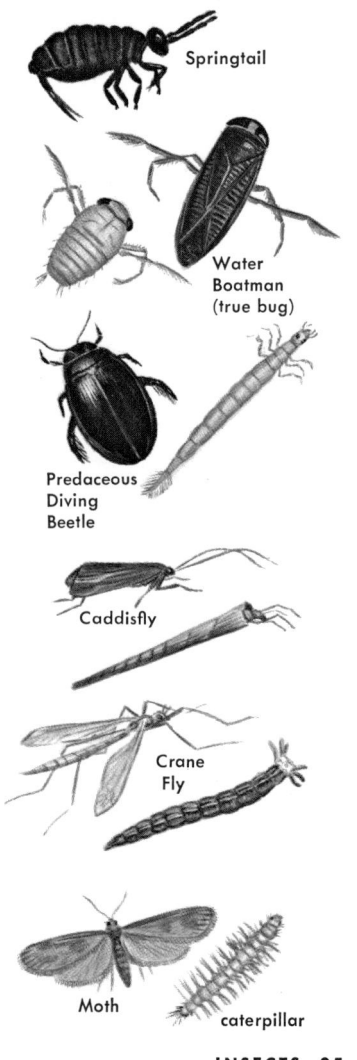

Springtail

TRUE BUGS (Hemiptera): both nymphs and adults are active predators. Nymphs have either one or no appendage at end of abdomen. In adults rear half of front wings is soft and membranous. Mouth is a beak for sucking. Pages 102-104.

Water Boatman (true bug)

BEETLES (Coleoptera): the larvae are active predators; they do not have appendages on abdomen but some have long tail filaments. Both larvae and adults have biting mouthparts. Adults have hard or leathery front wings. Some live only on the surface film of water others below. Pages 105-106.

Predaceous Diving Beetle

CADDISFLIES (Trichoptera): most larvae live in a case of leaves, sand grains, twigs, or other debris. Two tail hooks anchor them in case. Page 107.

Caddisfly

FLIES (Diptera): aquatic larvae are active, wormlike, legless. Pupae of most kinds are inactive, legs lacking (or inconspicuous); short, hard body sometimes in a case. Adults with one pair of wings. Pages 108-112.

Crane Fly

MOTHS (Lepidoptera): the larvae, or caterpillars, of a few species are aquatic, living under sheets of silk or under rocks. Biting mouthparts. Adults are dull in color. Page 112.

Moth

caterpillar

HEXAGENIAS, largest mayflies in N.A., are common in large lakes and rivers. Nymphs burrow into mud on bottom.

Hexagenia bilineata
2.5 in.

MAYFLIES (Ephemeroptera) have four nearly transparent wings held vertically when the insect is resting. Two or three long filaments project from the end of the abdomen. The aquatic nymphs (naiads) have rows of leaflike gills along the sides of the abdomen and, like the adults, three (sometimes two) long, usually feathery, tail appendages. Mayfly nymphs feed on small plants and animals and on organic debris. They live from a few months to three years in the water, depending on the species. At maturity they float to the surface, shed their skin, and transform into a flying, dull-colored subimago, or dun. This stage may last a day or more; then the subimago skin is shed and the shiny, sexually mature imago, or spinner, emerges. The adults of some species are truly ephemeral, living only a few hours. Adult mayflies take in no food; their nonfunctional mouthparts are greatly reduced in size. Adults mate in flight, countless millions sometimes involved in a nuptial swarming that often takes place near water. After her eggs are laid in the water, the female dies.

Both nymphs and adults are an important food of fishes. Mayflies are attracted to lights along shore, their bodies sometimes piling up a foot or more deep (p. 97, top). About 500 species occur in N.A.

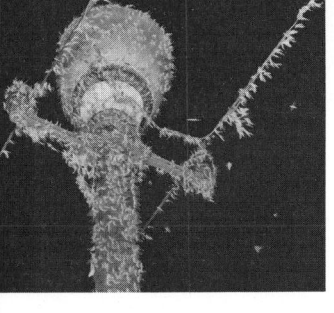

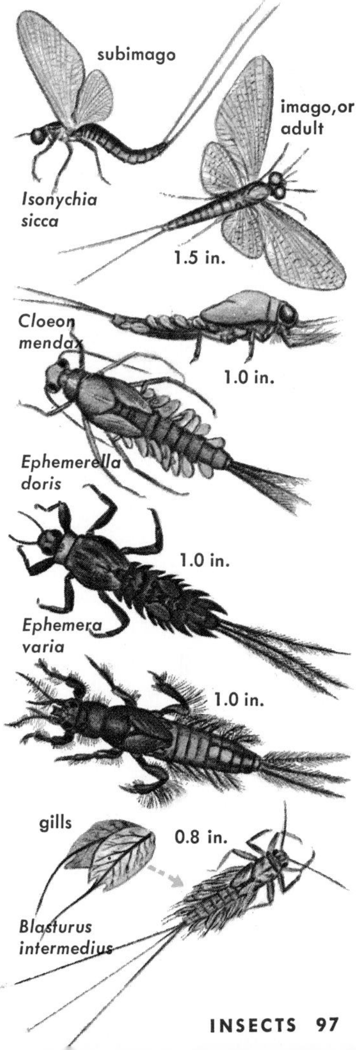

ISONYCHIA nymphs are adapted for life in flowing water and swim with quick, darting movements. Widely distributed.

CLOEON nymph is a climber, spending much time among plants. Found mainly in eastern and northern N.A.

EPHEMERELLA nymph is a sprawling type. It clings to objects on the bottom in ponds and streams. Gills are about half the width of the abdomen. Widely distributed in N.A.

EPHEMERA is common in small ponds. The nymphs burrow through bottom sediments. They keep their feathery gills in movement. This creates a current of water through the burrow, replenishing the oxygen for respiration.

BLASTURUS nymphs are abundant in small ponds in early spring. Their development is rapid so that by April or May they have matured and are gone. The nymphs are swift, darting types. Found in waters throughout most of N.A.

subimago

imago, or adult

Isonychia sicca

1.5 in.

Cloeon mendax

1.0 in.

Ephemerella doris

1.0 in.

Ephemera varia

1.0 in.

gills

0.8 in.

Blasturus intermedius

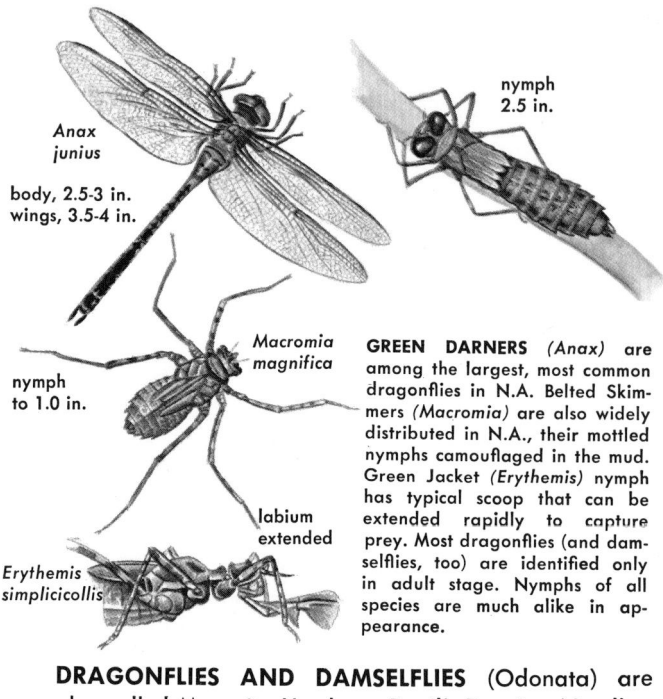

Anax
junius

body, 2.5-3 in.
wings, 3.5-4 in.

nymph
2.5 in.

Macromia
magnifica

nymph
to 1.0 in.

labium
extended

Erythemis
simplicicollis

GREEN DARNERS *(Anax)* are among the largest, most common dragonflies in N.A. Belted Skimmers *(Macromia)* are also widely distributed in N.A., their mottled nymphs camouflaged in the mud. Green Jacket *(Erythemis)* nymph has typical scoop that can be extended rapidly to capture prey. Most dragonflies (and damselflies, too) are identified only in adult stage. Nymphs of all species are much alike in appearance.

DRAGONFLIES AND DAMSELFLIES (Odonata) are also called Mosquito Hawks or Devil's Darning Needles. About 400 species occur in N.A. Dragonflies hold their wings in a horizontal position when at rest; the smaller, rather delicate damselflies hold their wings upward and backward. The nymphs of both are dull-colored, awkward-looking creatures with large chewing mouthparts covered by a scooplike lip (labium). The slim damselfly nymphs have three leaf-shaped gills at the tip of the abdomen. Dragonfly nymphs are broad and lack these gills. Both feed on insect larvae, worms, small crustaceans, or even small fishes. In turn, they are an important food of many larger fishes.

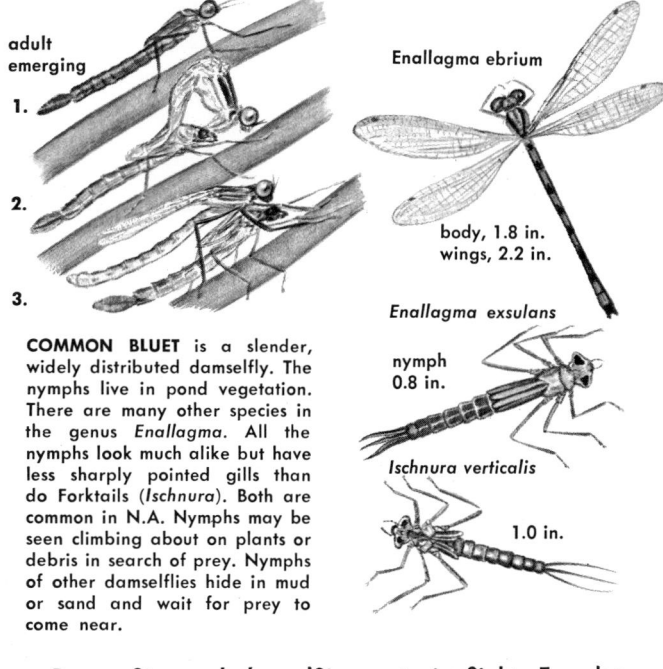

adult emerging

1.

2.

3.

Enallagma ebrium

body, 1.8 in.
wings, 2.2 in.

Enallagma exsulans

nymph
0.8 in.

Ischnura verticalis

1.0 in.

COMMON BLUET is a slender, widely distributed damselfly. The nymphs live in pond vegetation. There are many other species in the genus *Enallagma*. All the nymphs look much alike but have less sharply pointed gills than do Forktails (*Ischnura*). Both are common in N.A. Nymphs may be seen climbing about on plants or debris in search of prey. Nymphs of other damselflies hide in mud or sand and wait for prey to come near.

Dragonflies and damselflies mate in flight. Females deposit their eggs in the water, in floating plant masses, in sand, or in holes cut by the females in plant stems—the place and method of laying eggs varying with the species. Some species complete their life cycle from egg to adult in three months; others may take up to five years and pass through many nymphal stages before becoming adults. Transformation from nymph to adult (imago) takes place on a piling, on a plant stem sticking out from the water, or on some similar object. The nymph's outer skin splits lengthwise on the upper surface and the adult emerges. It must wait for its wings to dry before it can fly.

STONEFLIES (Plecoptera) have clear, membranous wings and long antennae. There are about 300 species in N.A. The nymphs live primarily in flowing waters but are found occasionally in quiet pools, usually under stones, leaves, or other bottom debris. They are sprawling creatures, up to 2 inches long, and have tufts of gills behind each leg. Some species feed on animals, others on plants. Fishes and other water animals feed on the stonefly nymphs.

SPRINGTAILS (Collembola), though not truly aquatic, are commonly found on the surface of ponds and in damp debris along water's edge. These primitive wingless insects, less than 0.2 inch long, jump by using a springing device under their abdomen.

ALDERFLIES, DOBSONS, AND FISHFLIES (Megaloptera) are active mostly at dusk or at night. Alderfly larvae are brownish, thick-skinned, and about 1 inch long. They are secretive, living mainly in mud or underneath stones in the shore zones. Dobsons are brownish with white-splotched wings measuring up to 5 inches in spread. Males have large curved mandibles used in clasping the females in mating. The predaceous larvae, called hellgrammites, may be as long as 3 inches. Fishflies are reddish-tan, often with yellowish streaks; wings brownish. The predaceous larvae resemble hellgrammites but are not as large.

SPONGILLA FLIES (Neuroptera), grayish or yellowish-brown, appear in summer and live only a few days. The larvae live on or in fresh-water sponges and feed on the sponge tissues. Spongilla flies (about 6 species in N.A.) are not well known.

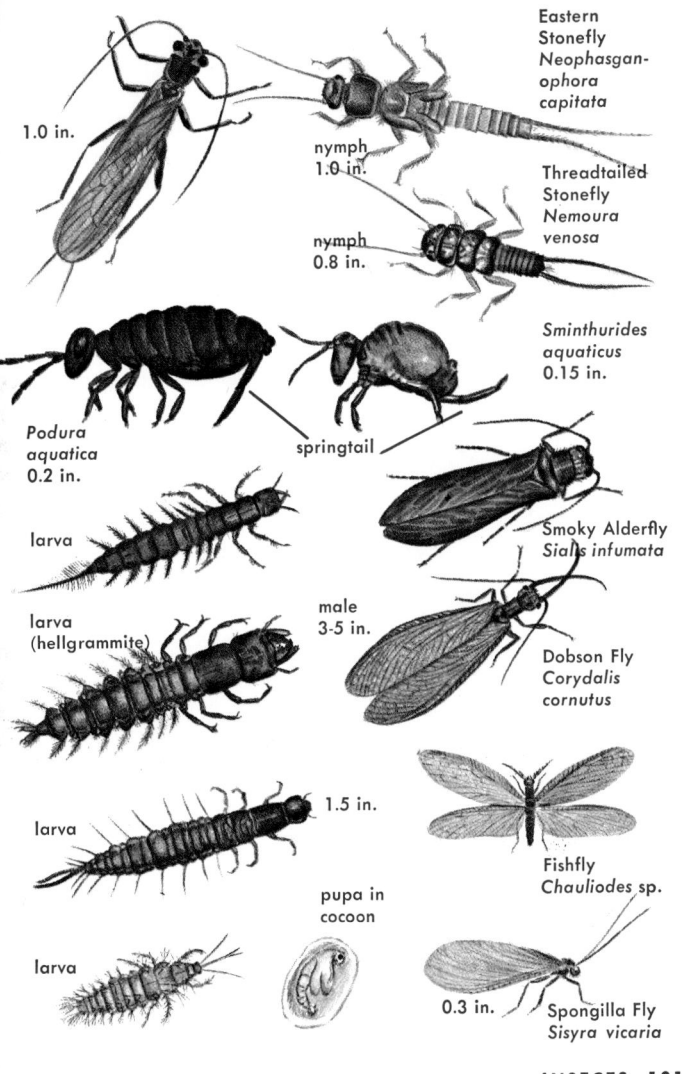

Eastern Stonefly
Neophasganophora capitata

1.0 in.

nymph 1.0 in.

Threadtailed Stonefly
Nemoura venosa

nymph 0.8 in.

Sminthurides aquaticus
0.15 in.

Podura aquatica
0.2 in.

springtail

larva

Smoky Alderfly
Sialis infumata

larva (hellgrammite)

male 3-5 in.

Dobson Fly
Corydalis cornutus

larva

1.5 in.

Fishfly
Chauliodes sp.

larva

pupa in cocoon

0.3 in.

Spongilla Fly
Sisyra vicaria

TRUE BUGS (Hemiptera) have mouthparts fitted for piercing and sucking. Some are wingless, but most kinds have four wings. The rear half of each front wing is membranous, and there is a triangular plate, the scutellum, between the wing bases. Young bugs are like miniature adults but lack wings. These nymphs change (metamorphose) gradually. Most aquatic bugs feed on insects or on other invertebrate animals. Some can fly; others walk on the surface. Most are adapted for swimming, diving, or clinging to underwater vegetation.

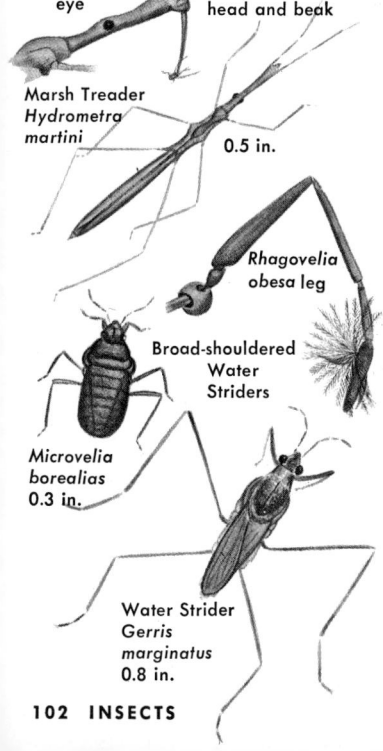

eye   head and beak

Marsh Treader
Hydrometra martini
0.5 in.

Rhagovelia obesa leg

Broad-shouldered
Water
Striders

Microvelia borealias
0.3 in.

Water Strider
Gerris marginatus
0.8 in.

MARSH TREADERS, or Water Measurers, are slender dark-colored bugs usually found creeping on the surface, especially in thick plant growths. They spear prey with their sharp beak, then suck out body juices. Eyes near base of long head. About 6 species known in N.A.

BROAD-SHOULDERED WATER STRIDERS are widest through the thorax, dark colored, and often have light markings. *Microvelia* is the common genus. Species of *Rhagovelia* use hairy tufts on middle legs as a paddle. Broad-shouldered Water Striders catch other insects or small crustaceans just beneath or on the surface. About 20 N.A. species.

WATER STRIDERS, or Pond Skaters, are slender, dark, long-legged bugs that skate or jump about on the surface film. Often they congregate in large numbers. Adults are usually wingless. Like the Broad-shouldered Water Striders, they are predaceous. About 30 species in N.A., nearly a third in the genus *Gerris*.

WATER TREADERS, small and commonly greenish, live on the surface near shore and on debris. They feed on animals found on the surface. Three species occur in N.A.

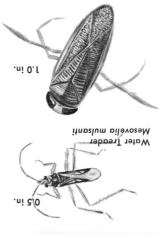

Water Treader
Mesovelia mulsanti

0.5 in.

WATER BOATMEN are slender bugs with long hind legs flattened for swimming. Air taken at the surface usually surrounds the insect in a silvery envelope. Water Boatmen must hold onto some object in order to remain submerged. Adults are strong fliers and commonly attracted to lights. They feed on algae or on decaying plant and animal matter sucked from bottom ooze. About 115 species of Water Boatmen are known in N.A. waters. *Arctocorixa* (here) and *Corixa* (p. 95) are two common genera.

Water Boatman
Arctocorixa interrupta

1.0 in.

WATER SCORPIONS have a breathing tube formed by two grooved filaments at the end of the abdomen. These bugs live underwater but project the breathing tube through the surface from time to time to replenish their air. They are carnivorous, seizing their prey with their strong front legs. About 12 species occur in N.A.

Water
Scorpion
*Ranatra
fusca*

2.5 in.

GIANT WATER BUGS are the largest of the true bugs. They feed on insects or even on tadpoles and small fishes, killing their prey with a poison secreted as they bite. In some species the male carries the eggs on his back. Attracted to lights. About 24 species in N.A.; most abundant in Southeast.

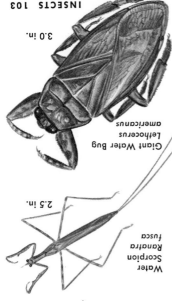

Giant Water Bug
*Lethocerus
americanus*

3.0 in.

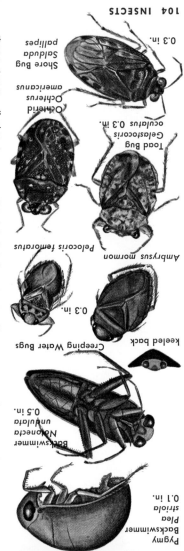

Shore Bug
Saldula
pallipes
0.3 in.

Ochterid
Ochterus
americanus

Toad Bug
Gelastocoris
oculatus 0.3 in.

Pelocoris femoratus

Ambrysus mormon

0.3 in.

Creeping Water Bugs

keeled back

Backswimmer
Notonecta
undulata
0.5 in.

Pygmy
Backswimmer
Plea
striola
0.1 in.

SHORE BUGS, or Saldids, are jumping bugs that live in the wet soil along shores throughout N.A. They fly quickly but only quickly but only suck juices from small dead invertebrates.

SHORE BUGS, or Saldids, are jumping bugs that live in the wet soil along shores throughout N.A. They fly quickly but only suck juices from small dead invertebrates.

TOAD BUGS are found in the mud and sand along shores of quiet waters over much of N.A. They have broad grasping front legs. Ochterids are similar to Toad Bugs, but they have slender front legs.

CREEPING WATER BUGS carry air in a bubble beneath their wings. They move by swimming and crawling, and grasp prey with their strong legs. Pelocoris occurs in eastern N.A.; Ambrysus is a western genus. About 20 species in N.A. Their bite is painful.

BACKSWIMMERS have a keeled, or boat-shaped, back and paddle-like legs. Their hind legs are much longer than the middle and front legs. Backswimmers hold a supply of air on the underside of the body and beneath the wings. They come to the surface periodically to rest and to replenish their air supply by sticking the tip of their abdomen above the surface. Their bite is painful. Only one species, widely distributed, occurs in N.A.

PYGMY BACKSWIMMERS are commonly found clinging in tangled masses of plants. They swim only short distances—from one plant to another. Their food consists mainly of small crustaceans. Only one species, widely distributed, occurs in N.A.

BEETLES (Coleoptera) have thick, heavy front wings that cover the membranous hind wings. Both the adults and the larvae have chewing mouthparts. Some feed on plants, others on animals; some are scavengers. Of about 280,000 species of beetles, only a few live in water during one or all of their four life stages. Beetle larvae are active; they have three pairs of legs.

PREDACEOUS DIVING BEETLES are common in most lakes and ponds. Both the larvae, often called Water Tigers, and the adults feed on insects or on other small water animals. Adults commonly hang head down with the tip of their abdomen above the surface. In this position they trap air beneath their wings. The shiny, brownish-black adults are strong fliers, frequently attracted to lights. More than 300 species are found in N.A.

CRAWLING WATER BEETLES live in shallow water among plant masses, especially algae. They are poor swimmers. The larvae eat only plants, but the adults eat both plants and animals. About 50 species in N.A.

WHIRLIGIG BEETLES use their short, fan-shaped middle and hind legs in skimming over the surface and in diving. Their front legs are long and slender. Each eye is divided into two parts so that the beetle sees above and beneath the water at the same time. The adults are scavengers; the larvae are voracious carnivores. More than 50 species in N.A. Many give off a strong odor when caught.

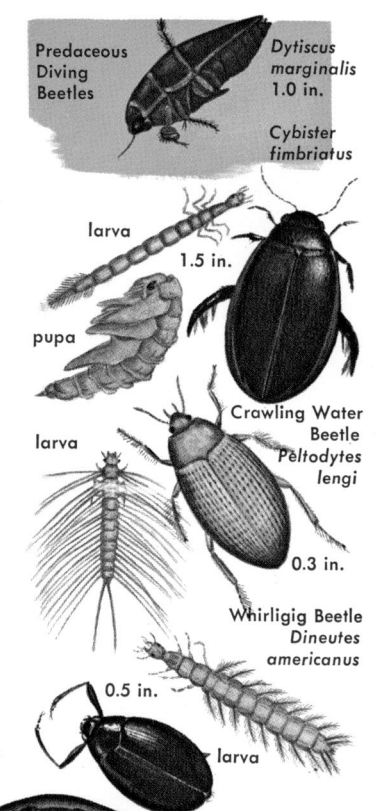

Predaceous Diving Beetles

Dytiscus marginalis 1.0 in.

Cybister fimbriatus

larva

1.5 in.

pupa

Crawling Water Beetle *Peltodytes lengi*

larva

0.3 in.

Whirligig Beetle *Dineutes americanus*

0.5 in.

larva

eyes

WATER SCAVENGER BEETLES have stubby, club-shaped antennae, which they stick above the surface when they need to replenish their air supply. The air is trapped on the antennae and under the wings. Adults are mainly vegetarians; the larvae, carnivorous. About 160 species occur in N.A. They range in length from 0.3 to 1.5 inches.

DRYOPIDS are small hairy beetles that feed on algae. Little is known about the larvae which cling to the undersides of sticks and stems. Adults are widely distributed in lakes, ponds, and streams. About 25 species are found in N.A.

ELMIDS crawl about over the bottom or on plants on which they feed. A film of air surrounding the adult's body serves as a reservoir of oxygen. About 75 eastern N.A. species.

LEAF BEETLES are mainly terrestrial, but some species are common on pond surfaces and feed on plants. Larvae breathe through two spiny tubes that tap air chambers of plant stem on which they are feeding. Full-grown larvae spin cocoons.

TIGER BEETLES of several species live along the wet, sandy shores of ponds, lakes, and streams. The attractive adults are active during the day and fly quickly when approached. The ugly, big-jawed larvae live in burrows and wait at the entrance for prey to come close enough for them to grab.

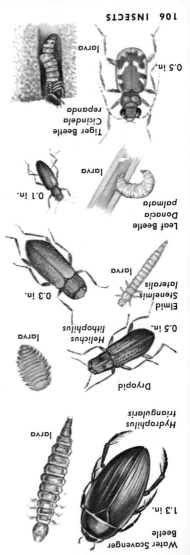

Tiger Beetle
Cicindela repanda
0.5 in.
larva

larva

Leaf Beetle
Donacia palmata
0.1 in.

Elmid
Stenelmis lateralis
larva
0.3 in.

Dryopid
Helichus lithophilus
0.5 in.
larva

Water Scavenger Beetle
Hydrophilus triangularis
1.3 in.
larva

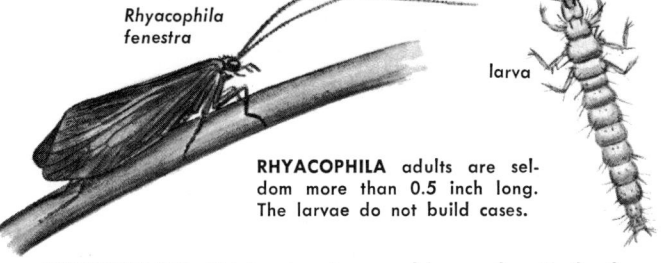

Rhyacophila fenestra

larva

RHYACOPHILA adults are seldom more than 0.5 inch long. The larvae do not build cases.

CADDISFLIES (Trichoptera) resemble moths. Both the larvae and pupae are aquatic. The soft-bodied larvae have a hard, horny covering on the head, and each of the three distinct segments of the thorax bears a pair of legs. Larvae of most live in tubelike cases of leaves, sand, twigs, or bark, so distinctive that most species can be identified by the type of case made. A few of the many kinds are shown below. Larvae that build portable cases pull them behind as they crawl about over the bottom. Larvae feed on both animals and plants. Some stream species build nets in which they capture food drifting in the water. Most of a caddisfly's life is spent as a larva. The pupal stage lasts about two weeks; the adult lives about a month. Caddisfly larvae are an important food of fishes, particularly trout. More than 750 species occur in N.A.

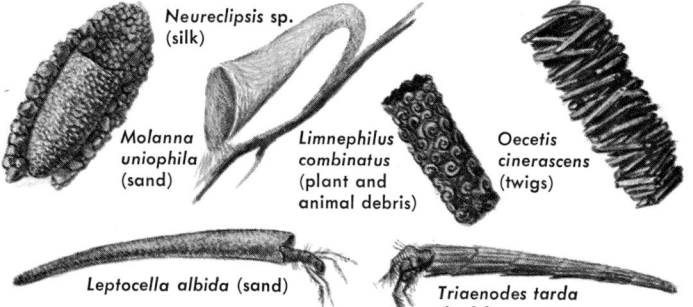

Neureclipsis sp. (silk)

Molanna uniophila (sand)

Limnephilus combinatus (plant and animal debris)

Oecetis cinerascens (twigs)

Leptocella albida (sand)

Triaenodes tarda (leaf fragments)

FLIES (Diptera) have one pair of transparent, nearly veinless front wings; the hind wings are reduced to stubby balancing organs, or halteres. Flies have lapping or piercing-sucking mouthparts, and in some, such as mosquitoes, they form a long proboscis. The larvae and pupae of many flies are aquatic, but no adults live in water. Though usually inconspicuous, the larvae may exist in large numbers in lakes and ponds, some at the surface and others in bottom debris and mud. They are an important food of fishes and other animals. The larval stage of some species lasts for only a few weeks; in others, for several years. Most fly larvae, or maggots, do not have a distinct head. They lack eyes.

MOSQUITO larvae, or wrigglers, range from 0.2 to more than 0.5 inch long. They differ from other fly larvae in that their head and thorax are larger than the remainder of the body. Mosquito larvae eat microscopic plants and animals or organic debris filtered through brushes that surround their mouth. They breathe through gills at the end of the abdomen. Larvae usually rest at surface, but wriggle downward if disturbed.

Mosquito pupae, commonly called tumblers, are also aquatic. Unlike those of the larvae, their head and thorax are fused into one unit, and they breathe through tubes in their thorax. In contrast to the pupae of most other insects, they are active and can swim by using their leaflike tail appendages.

Only the female mosquitoes are bloodsuckers. Many require a meal of blood before they are able to lay their eggs. Some kinds of mosquitoes transmit diseases, such as malaria and yellow fever. The males feed on nectar and ripe fruit. Mosquitoes survive winter and periods of drought in the egg stage, hatching as soon as conditions are favorable. About 120 species of mosquitoes occur in N.A.

PHANTOM GNATS resemble mosquitoes and, like them, have hairy, scaly wings. But adults do not feed, hence do not bite. They often appear in large, bothersome numbers and are attracted to lights. The larvae, about 0.5 inch long and nearly transparent, live in pools, ponds, and lakes. They swim and dart rapidly, preying on mosquito larvae, small crustaceans, and other small animals. The larvae's antennae, used in capturing prey and also in swimming, project downward in front of mouth.

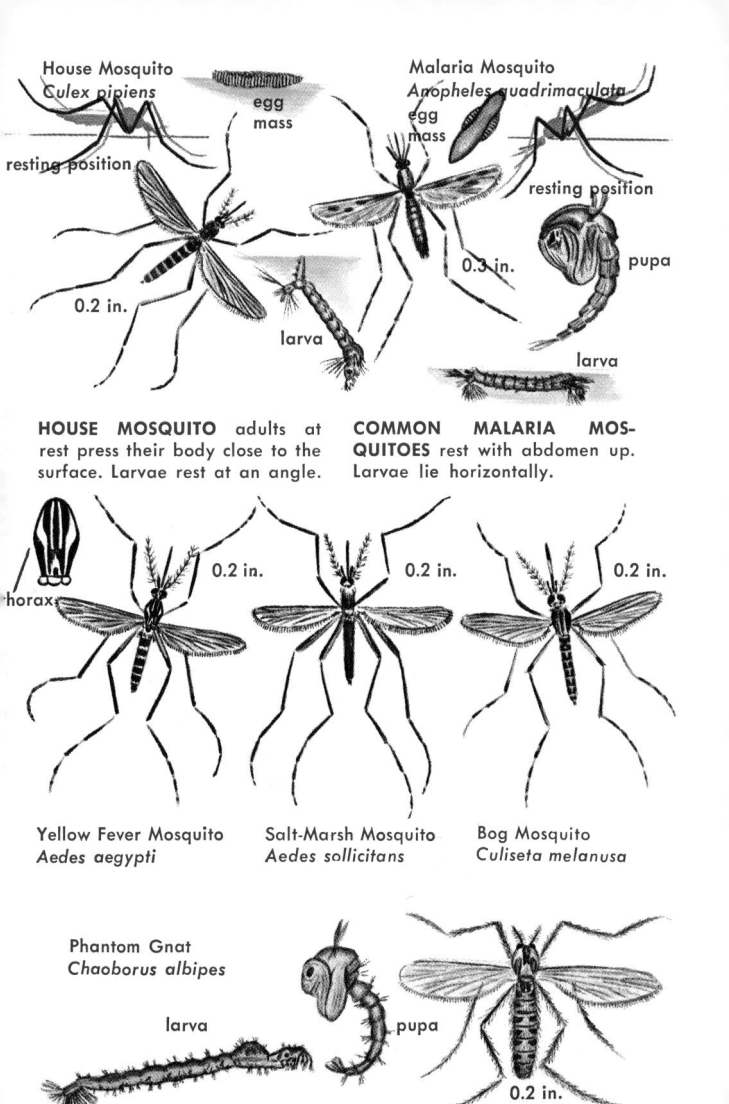

House Mosquito
Culex pipiens

egg mass

resting position

0.2 in.

larva

Malaria Mosquito
Anopheles quadrimaculata

egg mass

resting position

pupa

0.3 in.

larva

HOUSE MOSQUITO adults at rest press their body close to the surface. Larvae rest at an angle.

COMMON MALARIA MOSQUITOES rest with abdomen up. Larvae lie horizontally.

thorax

0.2 in.

0.2 in.

0.2 in.

Yellow Fever Mosquito
Aedes aegypti

Salt-Marsh Mosquito
Aedes sollicitans

Bog Mosquito
Culiseta melanusa

Phantom Gnat
Chaoborus albipes

larva

pupa

0.2 in.

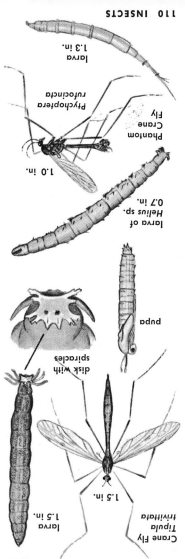

larva 1.3 in.

Phantom Crane Fly

Ptychoptera rufocincta

1.0 in.

larva of *Helius* sp. 0.7 in.

pupa

disk with spiracles

Crane Fly *Tipula trivittata*

1.5 in.

larva 1.5 in.

CRANE FLIES look like giant mosquitoes. Widely distributed in N.A., they are commonly found swarming near ponds and are also attracted to lights. Crane flies mate in flight, and the females lay their eggs in water. The brownish to whitish aquatic larvae can be recognized by the disk at the end of their tail. This disk, which has tubelike spiracles, is thrust through the surface for breathing. Some crane fly larvae are predaceous; others are vegetarian. Adults of some species feed on nectar, but the adults of many species do not eat. Craneflies do not bite.

About 30 species of N.A. crane flies are aquatic. Among the most widely distributed are the species of *Tipula*. Their large tough-skinned larvae, sometimes called Leather Jackets, live in mats of algae or other vegetation, in the sandy or muddy bottoms of lakes, and ponds, in wet grass, or in debris of lowland shores. Species of *Helius* live in rich muds and on floating vegetation in marshes, especially in waters where emergent plants are abundant.

PHANTOM CRANE FLIES resemble true crane flies. Unlike the larvae of true crane flies, the larvae have a long respiratory tube at the rear. Phantom crane fly larvae live in decaying plants and in mud at the edge of ponds and lakes. Air sacs on the feet of adults of some species aid in a "ballooning" or "kiting" flight in even slight winds. Only 6 species in N.A.

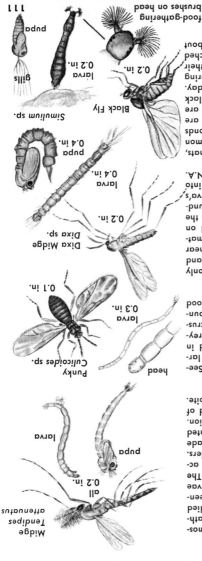

TRUE MIDGES resemble mosquitoes. Males have large, feathery antennae. The round-bodied larvae are red, yellowish, greenish, or whitish colored. Red larvae are called "bloodworms." The pupae of many species are active, like mosquito tumblers. Some species live in tubes made of sand, silt, or debris cemented together with a sticky secretion. Larvae are an important food of fishes. Most adults do not bite. About 200 N.A. species.

PUNKIES (Sand Flies or No-See-Ums) are biting midges. The larvae live in plant masses and in mud. They are carnivorous, preying on small insects and crustaceans. They may be very abundant and are an important food of small fishes.

DIXA MIDGES are commonly seen at sundown dancing up and down in flight over and near bodies of water. These are matting swarms. The larvae feed on microscopic food filtered from the water through brushes surrounding their mouth. At rest a larva's body, like pupa's, is bent into a "U." About 8 species in N.A.

BLACK FLIES, or Buffalo Gnats, are small flies more common near streams than around ponds and lakes. The females are bloodsuckers, and their bites are painful. Unlike mosquitoes, black flies are active during the day. The larvae have food-gathering brushes on each side of their head. Masses of larvae attached to stones look like moss. About 50 species in N.A.

Midge *Tendipes attenuatus* all 0.2 in.

larva

pupa

Punky *Culicoides* sp. 0.3 in. larva 0.1 in. head

Dixa Midge *Dixa* sp. 0.2 in. larva 0.4 in. pupa 0.4 in.

Black Fly 0.2 in. food-gathering brushes on head larva 0.2 in. *Simulium* sp. pupa gills

Horse Fly
Tabanus atratus
0.9 in.

Deer Fly
Chrysops callidus

0.4 in.

larva
1.0 in.

Drone Fly
Eristalis tenax

larva
1.5 in.

0.5 in.

breathing tube

0.4 in.

Soldier Fly
Stratiomyia sp.

larva
1.2 in.

HORSE FLY and Deer Fly larvae (many species) are aquatic. Robust and wormlike, horse fly larvae are about 1 inch long and tapered at both ends. Deer fly larvae are smaller. Both prey on worms, snails, and other animals. Females lay eggs on plants or rocks just above water surface. Female flies bite; males feed on nectar.

DRONE FLY larvae, called rat-tailed maggots, live in debris on the bottom in shallow waters. They breathe through a tube, as much as 1 inch long, that sticks above surface. Drone Flies are members of the flower fly family, important pollinators.

SOLDIER FLIES include a few species with aquatic larvae. Some are nearly 2 inches long. Stiff and covered with a thick skin, they appear lifeless. Hairlike setae surround breathing spiracles at end of abdomen.

MOTHS, the largest group of Lepidoptera, include a few aquatic species. The caterpillars are about 0.8 inch long. Some build silk-lined cases of leaf fragments. In other species the pupae develop in cases attached to underwater plants; still others attach the cases to plants above the water. The small moths of these aquatic species are dull brown or gray.

Nymphula maculalis

larva in leaf case

0.9 in.

larva
0.8 in.

pupa

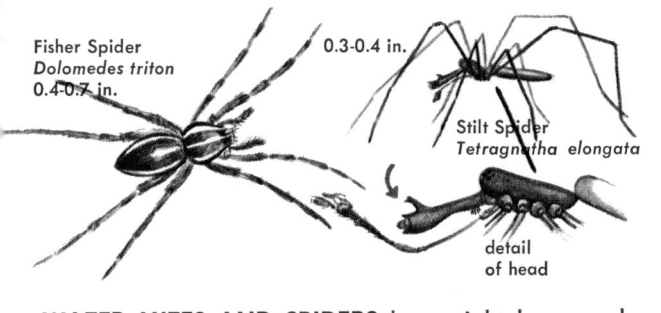

Fisher Spider
Dolomedes triton
0.4-0.7 in.

0.3-0.4 in.

Stilt Spider
Tetragnatha elongata

detail
of head

WATER MITES AND SPIDERS have eight legs, as do ticks, scorpions, and other members of the same arthropod group—Arachnida.

Among the few kinds of spiders that spend their life in or near the water is the Fisher Spider, which can dive and remain submerged for long periods. Widespread in N.A., it feeds mainly on insects but has been known also to catch small fishes and tadpoles. The Stilt Spider, an orb weaver, lives near shores of ponds and streams and often skates across water. It catches midges, crane flies, and other insects in its snare. Many other kinds of spiders may be found under logs or rocks or in the vegetation along shores.

Water mites, usually no more than 0.2 inch long, live with the floating plankton or in wet vegetation along shores. Each species is usually restricted to a particular habitat. Water mites feed on worms, small crustaceans, and insects; some are parasites. A few swim; others crawl about on plants or rocks; all surface to get air.

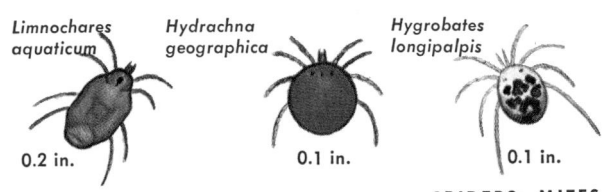

Limnochares aquaticum

Hydrachna geographica

Hygrobates longipalpis

0.2 in.

0.1 in.

0.1 in.

MOLLUSKS are soft-bodied animals, their soft parts surrounded by a shell. (Exceptions are the land-dwelling slugs and the marine squids and octopuses, in which the shell is absent or small and internal.) The two groups represented in fresh water are snails and clams. In both, the shells are composed largely of lime secreted by the fleshy tissue (mantle) surrounding the animal's body. Mollusks are not abundant in soft or acid waters (those with a low pH), in which their limy shells would dissolve.

SNAILS (Gastropoda) typically have a single coiled shell that may be rounded, flattened, or highly spired. Snails have a distinct head with a pair of sensory tentacles that can be extended or retracted. An eye is located at the base of each tentacle. Beneath the tentacles is the mouth, equipped with a rasping tongue, the radula, that is worked back and forth like a file to shred food. Fresh-water snails feed mainly on plants, though some eat dead animals. They are food themselves of many different kinds of fishes and a few kinds of birds and animals. Some are the hosts of parasitic worms. Snails crawl on a thick, muscular "foot" on the underside of their body.

GILLED SNAILS, or Prosobranchs, breathe by means of a gill, a set of leaflike tissues on the mantle. A thin, horny plate, the operculum, is attached to the "foot" and seals the opening to the shell when the foot is retracted.

Nearly all gilled snails lay their eggs in jelly-like cocoons. In winkles, however, the eggs are held inside the adult's shell until they hatch.

PULMONATE SNAILS have a sac-like "lung," formed from a portion of the mantle. They breathe air at the water surface, but some can stay underwater indefinitely, respiration taking place through body surface. Pulmonate snails do not have an operculum to close shell opening. Most species lay their eggs in gelatinous masses on submerged stones or plants.

GILLED SNAILS

PULMONATE SNAILS

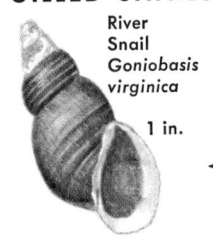

River
Snail
*Goniobasis
virginica*

1 in.

Shells cone-shaped. Widespread in N.A.; only abundant locally. ►

Fresh-water
Limpet
*Ferrissia
rivularis*
0.3 in.

Some shells rough, others smooth. Found from Conn. to Va. ◄

0.3 in.

Hairy Wheel Snail
Gyraulus hirsutus

Little Pond
Snail
*Amnicola
limnosa*
0.3 in.

Most N.A. still waters. Hairlike shell covering. ►

0.4 in.

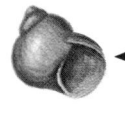

Ponds and streams, most abundant east of Rockies.

Orb Snail
*Helisoma
anceps*

1.5 in.

Common species of quiet waters. Many N.A. relatives. ►

Winkle
*Viviparus
intertextus*

Found in mud-bottomed waters of eastern N.A. ◄

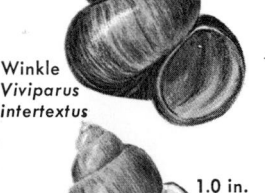

1.0 in.

Introduced from Europe; now spreading in the East. ►

Eared
Pond Snail
Lymnaea auricularis

1.5 in.

Pointed
Winkle

Shell thick. Many related species, all from eastern N.A. ◄

*Campeloma
subsolidum*

Giant Pond Snail
*Lymnaea
stagnalis*

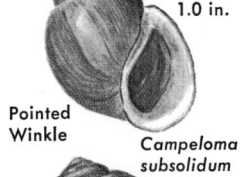

Shells usually thin. Quiet waters of middle N.A., also Europe and Asia.

Largest N.A. snail, from ponds and ditches of south-eastern U.S. ▼

Apple Snail
Pomacea paludosa

2 in.

2.5 in.

CLAMS (Pelecypoda) include species that live in mud and sand of ponds, lakes, and streams. They are especially abundant in the waters of the Mississippi Valley, but they are rare in water deeper than six feet. Unlike snails, clams do not have a head, radula, or tentacles. Two openings (siphons) are located at one end of their bivalved shell. One siphon takes in water, which contains food and dissolved oxygen; the water pumped out the other siphon carries away wastes. The fertile eggs of clams are retained in a special chamber of the adult until they hatch. Adults of some species may contain more than three million developing embryos. Glochidia, larvae of fresh-water clams, or mussels, cling to gills or fins of fishes. They live as parasites for a while before dropping off and settling to the bottom.

Many kinds of fishes feed on small, thin-shelled clams. Mink, raccoons, and some turtles can open those with thick shells to eat the soft insides.

FRESH-WATER CLAMS probably evolved from a salt-water form into fresh water.

Some freshwater bivalves have a larval stage, the glochidium, which clings as a parasite to fins of fishes.

Lines, or rings, on the outside of a clam's shell are growth marks. Inside, the hinge can be seen.

Clams dig in mud or sand with their wedge-shaped, "hatchet" foot. Water passes in and out the shell cavity through the tubelike siphons.

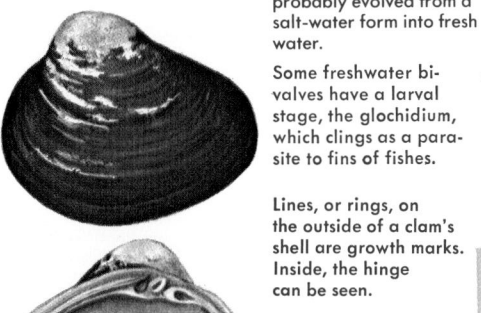

glochidium detail

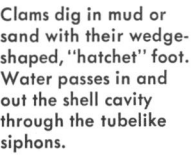
siphons

foot

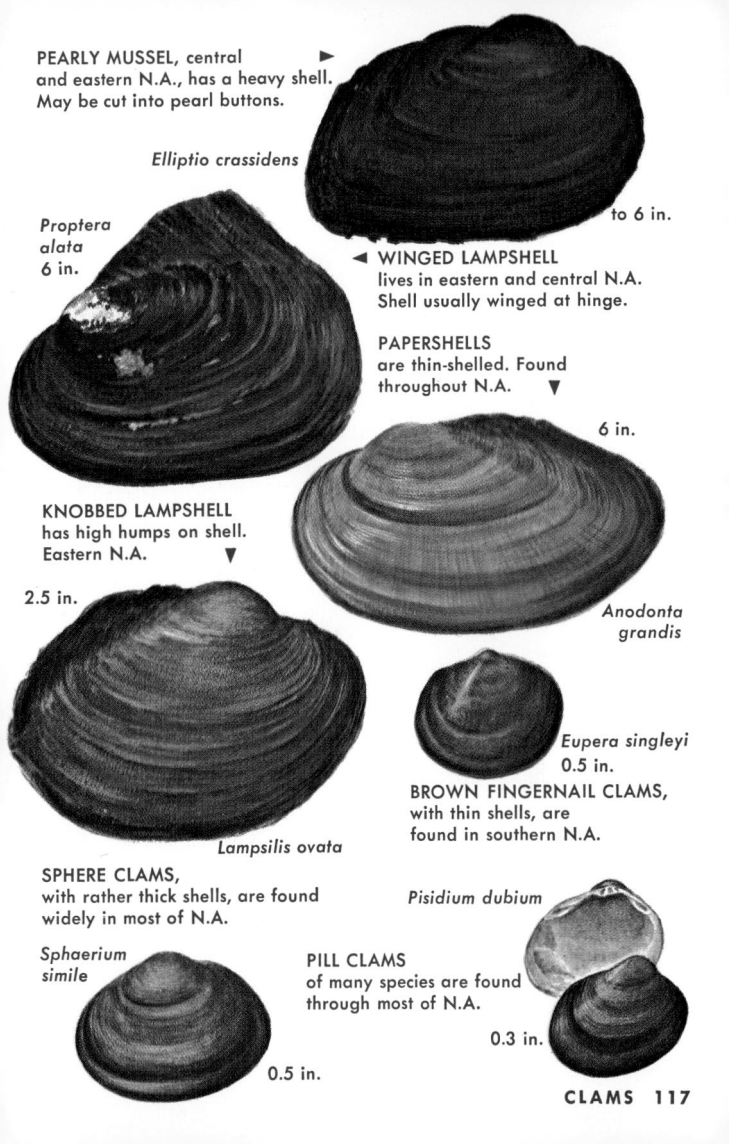

PEARLY MUSSEL, central
and eastern N.A., has a heavy shell.
May be cut into pearl buttons. ▶

Elliptio crassidens

to 6 in.

*Proptera
alata*
6 in.

◀ WINGED LAMPSHELL
lives in eastern and central N.A.
Shell usually winged at hinge.

PAPERSHELLS
are thin-shelled. Found
throughout N.A. ▼

6 in.

KNOBBED LAMPSHELL
has high humps on shell.
Eastern N.A. ▼

2.5 in.

*Anodonta
grandis*

Eupera singleyi
0.5 in.

BROWN FINGERNAIL CLAMS,
with thin shells, are
found in southern N.A.

Lampsilis ovata

SPHERE CLAMS,
with rather thick shells, are found
widely in most of N.A.

Pisidium dubium

*Sphaerium
simile*

PILL CLAMS
of many species are found
through most of N.A.

0.3 in.

0.5 in.

OTHER INVERTEBRATES from smaller groups are sometimes abundant in ponds and lakes. Most of these animals are not common, and little is known about their habits or the importance of their roles in the aquatic environment. Some kinds may appear in ponds and lakes only at certain seasons.

PROBOSCIS WORMS, or Nemerteans, are slender, unsegmented worms, sometimes called Ribbon Worms. Their soft, flat body is seldom more than 1 inch long. The long, extendible proboscis is sometimes two or three times longer than the animal's body. Nemerteans creep along on plant debris and feed on small animals and algae. A single fresh-water species is widely distributed in N.A. and is found most abundantly in autumn. Many other species are marine.

NEMATODES or Nemas, are roundworms, usually abundant in the bottom mud and sand or in masses of debris in ponds and lakes. About 1,000 species are found in fresh waters. Usually less than 0.1 inch long, their distinctive feature is the constant whiplike thrashing motion that throws the body into the form of an "S." Some nematodes are parasites, infesting crustaceans or even other worms. Others are predatory, and many feed on plants.

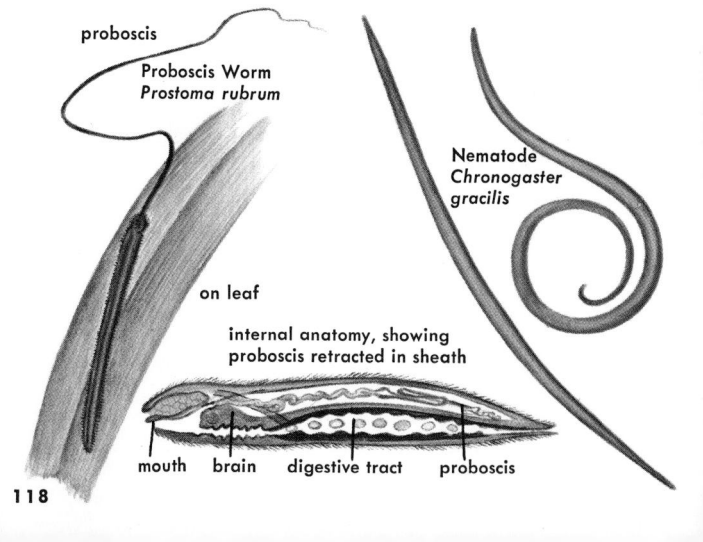

proboscis

Proboscis Worm
Prostoma rubrum

Nematode
Chronogaster gracilis

on leaf

internal anatomy, showing proboscis retracted in sheath

mouth   brain   digestive tract   proboscis

GASTROTRICHS are microscopic animals that live in bottom debris attached by a secretion from their tail appendages. About 60 percent of the approximately 200 species live in fresh water. Primarily algae eaters. *Chaetonotus* is an example.

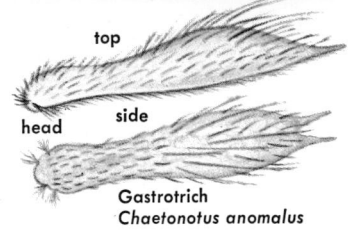

top

head   side

Gastrotrich
Chaetonotus anomalus

HORSEHAIR WORMS, common in quiet waters in summer, are long (to about 40 inches), cylindrical worms with a wiry, hairlike body and a blunt head. Females lay strings of eggs nearly 8 feet long. The larvae are parasitic on crustaceans, insects, and mollusks. Often called Gordian Worms because the tangled masses of individuals suggest the mythical Gordian Knot. They are called Horsehair Worms because they look like horsehairs that have come alive.

WATER BEARS, or Tardigrades, live among sand grains of wet beaches and on plants in fresh waters. Less than 0.05 inch long, the body is composed of a head and four segments. Each of the four pairs of legs ends in several claws. During dry seasons, water bears shrivel and remain inactive or dormant until moisture returns. They eat plants and are prey themselves of one-celled and other small animals. About 40 species of water bears occur in N.A. waters.

Water Bear
Hysibius sp.

Horsehair Worms
Gordius sp.

underside

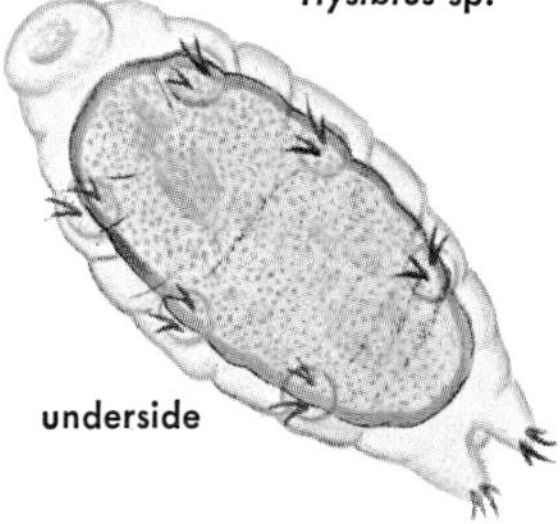

VERTEBRATES—fishes, amphibians, reptiles, birds, and mammals—are the largest and best known animals. Numerous species are adapted to fresh-water and wetland life. No attempt has been made to cover all orders and families of backboned animals. A variety are illustrated, for these animals are an important part of the total pond life picture.

LAMPREYS are primitive fishes with skeletons of cartilage rather than of bone. They are eel-like in shape and in manner of swimming. Their circular mouth lacks movable jaws. About 10 species of lampreys live in the streams and lakes of southern Canada and from the Mississippi eastward. One species occurs on the Pacific Coast. Most are small; some are parasitic on larger fishes. The large Sea Lamprey invaded the Great Lakes from the sea several years ago and has destroyed the Lake Trout commercial fishing industry.

AMERICAN BROOK LAMPREY is common in trout streams and sometimes in ponds. The larvae feed on organic debris. Adults, about 8 inches long, eat little. They are found in waters of central and eastern N.A.

American Brook Lamprey
Entosphenus lampetra

toothed, rasping mouth

SEA LAMPREY spends three or more years as a larva in streams feeding lakes. Grows to 3 feet long.

Lake Trout

Sea Lamprey
Petromyzon marinus

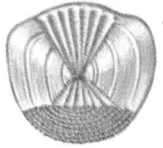

cycloid—smooth at rear

ctenoid—spiny at rear

Both types of scales shown here overlap like shingles. Ctenoids are found on sunfishes and similar spiny-rayed fishes; cycloids, on trout and other soft-rayed fishes.

BONY FISHES The typical bony fish has scales embedded in its skin, fins supported by rays, and a streamlined body. As water passes in the mouth and then out over the gills, oxygen dissolved in the water is exchanged for carbon dioxide from the fish's blood. A fish's scales have concentric ridges. Rapid growth results in widely spaced ridges; reduced growth in winter causes them to be close together. Growth rings can be counted to determine a fish's age.

Some fishes feed on algae and other plants. Young fishes and some adults eat large quantities of small invertebrates. Others, such as bass and pickerel, prey on tadpoles, fishes, and other large water animals.

Common fishes are shown here. For others, see Golden Nature Guide *Fishes*.

BROOK TROUT, in the salmon family, have white on front edge of fins. Native to cold waters of eastern N.A. but now widely stocked. Average 0.2 pound; rarely to 10.

RAINBOW TROUT feed on insects, mollusks, crustaceans, and fishes. Native to western N.A. but introduced to cold eastern waters. Average 2 pounds but may reach 40.

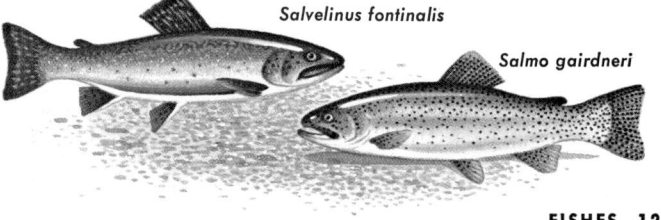

Salvelinus fontinalis

Salmo gairdneri

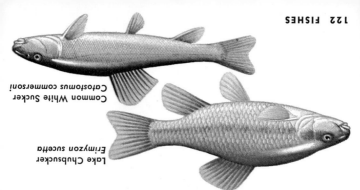

Comon White Sucker
Catostomus commersoni

Lake Chubsucker
Erimyzon sucetta

LAKE CHUBSUCKER, found in quiet waters from the Great Lakes to Texas and eastward, has a red tailfin when young. Lake Chubsuckers grub in bottom mud for insects and other organisms. Spawn in early spring, females scattering eggs over bottom. To 1 pound.

COMMON WHITE SUCKERS live in small to large lakes and in streams throughout central and eastern N.A. Their food consists of insect larvae, other small animals, and plants that are sucked in as the fish feed along the bottom. When full grown, 1 to 1.5 pounds.

REDHORSE, also a sucker, is common in lakes and sluggish streams in central and most of eastern N.A. Usually weighs 1 pound or less but sometimes reaches 8 pounds. In some regions the Redhorse is prized as an edible catch.

BUFFALO belong to the sucker family, with some 60 species in N.A. Most are bottom feeders, eating mollusks, insects, and plants. Bigmouth Buffalo grows to 65 pounds, though usually smaller. Mouth directed upward, not down as in suckers.

Northern Redhorse
Moxostoma macrolepidotum

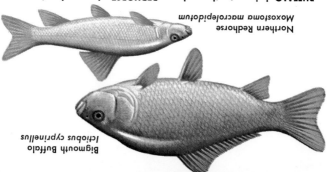

Bigmouth Buffalo
Ictiobus cyprinellus

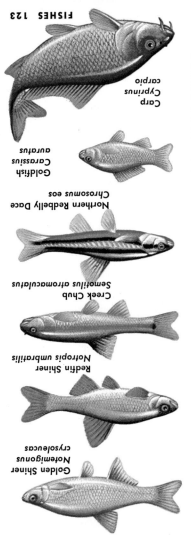

Carp
*Cyprinus
carpio*

Goldfish
*Carassius
auratus*

Northern Redbelly Dace
Chrosomus eos

Creek Chub
Semotilus atromaculatus

Redfin Shiner
Notropis umbratilis

Golden Shiner
*Notemigonus
crysoleucas*

CARP AND GOLDFISH, also members of the minnow family, are not native to N.A. The Carp, a native of Asia, was introduced to N.A. from Europe about 1870. The Goldfish was also a native of Asia. Both have been widely distributed. Carp commonly weigh 20 pounds and are omnivorous feeders. Goldfish found in the wild are those freed from fish bowls. They soon lose their color, becoming white or blotched.

REDBELLY DACE is one of the most common minnows in acid waters of bogs and ponds throughout central and eastern N.A. It feeds mainly on algae and plant debris. Reaches a length of about 3 inches.

CREEK CHUB is a large minnow, to about 10 inches long. It is common in streams and in some lakes and ponds throughout central and eastern N.A. Often caught on hook and line. Their food consists mostly of insects.

REDFIN SHINERS, about 3 inches long, occur in central and eastern N.A. Like the many other shiners, the Redfin is an important food link between plankton and large fishes.

GOLDEN SHINER, a member of the minnow family, is found throughout central and eastern N.A. Its food consists largely of algae and tiny animals. Shiners are commonly used as bait and as a food fish in hatcheries. Length to more than 12 inches.

GREEN SUNFISH is one of a dozen or so flat-sided, deep-bodied sunfish that are widespread in N.A. It feeds on insects and small crustaceans. Spawns in colonies in summer, the males fanning saucer-shaped nests in sand with fins. Average length 4 to 6 inches.

BLUEGILL SUNFISH is widely distributed as a result of stocking in farm ponds and other waters. Bluegills eat insects, crustaceans, and other small animals. A large female may lay more than 60,000 eggs at one spawning, but only a few of the many young survive. Length 8 to 12 inches; occasionally may weigh as much as 1 pound.

PUMPKINSEED SUNFISH is similar to Bluegill but has a bright red spot on each gill cover. It inhabits weedy waters in central and southern N.A., east of Rockies. Hybrids of Pumpkinseed with Green and Bluegill sunfish are difficult to identify.

WARMOUTH is found in quiet waters in central N.A. from the Mississippi eastward. It prefers mud-bottomed ponds and, like related sunfish, feeds largely on insects and small fishes. Length, 8 to 10 inches.

ORANGESPOTTED SUNFISH lives in quiet waters throughout central and eastern N.A. Most abundant in weedy spots near holes. Feeds on insects and crustaceans. Reaches a length of about 4 to 5 inches.

Green Sunfish
Lepomis cyanellus

Bluegill Sunfish
Lepomis macrochirus

Pumpkinseed
Lepomis gibbosus

Warmouth
Chaenobryttus gulosus

Orange-spotted Sunfish
Lepomis humilis

Johnny Darter
Etheostoma nigrum

Yellow Perch
Perca flavescens

YELLOW PERCH, of same family as Walleye, Sauger, and darters, live in ponds and lakes in cool regions of N.A. Found in deep waters during day, shallows at night. Feeds on smaller fishes, crustaceans, and other small animals. Length about 12 inches, weight 1 pound.

JOHNNY DARTER is one of about 100 species of darters, most of which are stream dwellers. Some are no more than 1 inch long; others reach a length of 5 inches. The male Johnny Darter and some other kinds of darters build nests and guard their eggs until they hatch.

LARGEMOUTH BASS, a large member of the sunfish family, is common in ponds, lakes, and sluggish streams throughout central and southern N.A. It preys on smaller fishes. The Largemouth Bass averages 2 to 4 pounds, but in the South grows to more than 18 pounds.

CRAPPIES are also large sunfish. Both the Black and the White are widely distributed in N.A. White Crappie has dark bars on sides but lives in murkier waters than Black. Both are carnivorous. They sometimes grow to 4 pounds, usually 1 to 2 pounds.

Largemouth Bass
Micropterus salmoides

White Crappie
Pomoxis annularis

Black Crappie
Pomoxis nigromaculatus

Banded Killifish
Fundulus diaphanus

Mosquitofish
male

Gambusia affinis

female

BANDED KILLIFISH, 3 to 4 inches long, is a topminnow, one of a large family found in fresh and salt waters. Head is flattened, mouth directed upward for surface feeding. Killifish feed on small plants and animals. Banded Killifish lives in northern waters. Hardy minnows can be kept for a long time in aquariums.

MOSQUITOFISH, or Gambusias, are about 2 inches long. They are topminnows, feeding at surface and introduced widely for mosquito control. Gambusias bear their young alive, breeding throughout the summer. Males are much smaller than females. They are native from southern N.A. southward.

PICKERELS are slender fishes of streams and quiet waters. They have flat, ducklike jaws and feed on fishes and other small animals. Some pickerels, especially Northern Pike and Muskellunge, are popular sport fish. All belong to the pike family.

AMERICAN EELS have tiny scales deep in the skin. They swim with snakelike movements and are most active at night. Eels feed on other fishes. May grow to 6 feet. They spawn at sea, and the young migrate up streams to ponds and lakes.

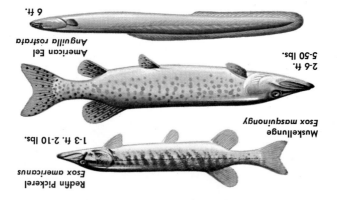

Redfin Pickerel
Esox americanus
1-3 ft. 2-10 lbs.

Muskellunge
Esox masquinongy
2-6 ft. 5-50 lbs.

American Eel
Anguilla rostrata
6 ft.

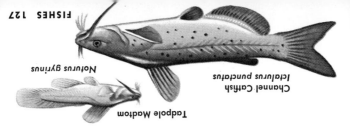

Channel Catfish
Ictalurus punctatus

Tadpole Madtom

Noturus gyrinus

BULLHEADS are found in ponds and sluggish streams throughout N.A. Like other catfish, bullheads have a smooth, scaleless skin and a sharp spine in the top (dorsal) fin and in each side (pectoral) fin. Chin whiskers, or barbels, are sensory organs that aid fish in finding food, primar-ily small bottom animals. Bull-heads and other catfish feed mostly at night or in roiled wat-ers; their eyes are small. Most common is Black Bullhead. Yel-low Bullhead inhabits clearer water than Brown or Black. All are good to eat. Average 0.5 to 1.0 pounds; 12 inches long.

TADPOLE MADTOMS, usually 3 to 4 inches long, are small cat-fish of quiet, weedy waters. Madtoms have a poison gland at the base of the spine in their pectoral fin and can inflict a painful wound. The small fatty (adipose) fin is joined to the tail fin, rather than free as in other catfish.

CHANNEL CATFISH, and most true catfish, are primarily stream dwellers, but Channel Catfish lives in lakes and has been stocked in ponds. Tail fin deeply notched. Spotted young are com-monly called "fiddlers." Catfish are edible and have firm flesh, especially when from cool wa-ters. Usually 2 to 4 pounds.

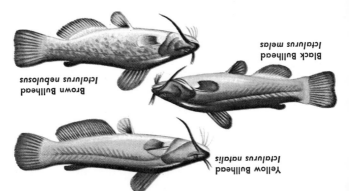

Brown Bullhead
Ictalurus nebulosus

Black Bullhead
Ictalurus melas

Yellow Bullhead
Ictalurus natalis

Gizzard Shad
*Dorosoma
cepedianum*

Longnose Gar
Lepisosteus osseus

GARS are long, slender, predatory fishes of quiet waters east of Rockies. They have sharp teeth and an armor of thick scales. Longnose Gar, 100 grows to 10 feet long, 100 pounds. Alligator Gar of South jaws twice as long as head, may be 5 feet long. Found in northern waters with Shortnose Gar. Spotted and Florida Gars are found only in southern waters.

GIZZARD SHAD belongs to herring family, which includes anchovies and other marine species. A plankton feeder, it strains food from water that passes through sievelike mesh of extensions, or rakers, on gills. Found in middle and eastern N.A., usually in large numbers. Gizzard Shad serves as food for larger species. Average 1 to 3 pounds.

LAKE STURGEON is one of several species of sturgeons in N.A. Sensitive feelers (barbels) aid in detecting small bottom-dwelling animals on which it feeds. Mouth protrudes as a tube. To 4 feet, 50 pounds.

BOWFINS, sometimes called Dog-fish, live in sluggish waters throughout eastern N.A. Highly carnivorous, they grow nearly 3 feet long. Easily recognized by long dorsal fin. Young guarded by adult. To 15 pounds.

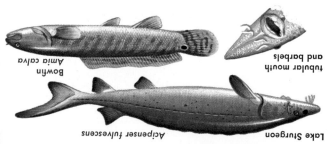

Bowfin
Amia calva

tubular mouth
and barbels

Lake Sturgeon

Acipenser fulvescens

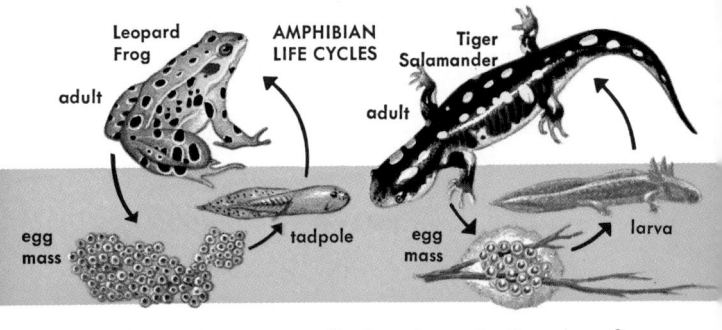

Leopard Frog — AMPHIBIAN LIFE CYCLES — Tiger Salamander

adult — adult

egg mass → tadpole — egg mass → larva

AMPHIBIANS are typically four-legged, though a few kinds lack one or both pairs. Frogs and toads do not have tails as adults; newts and salamanders do. Amphibians live mainly in water or in damp places, as their skin provides little protection against drying. In a typical life cycle, as illustrated above, there is a gilled larval stage that is wholly aquatic. Eventually the larva (those of frogs and toads are called tadpoles) develops into an adult. Some adult amphibians live on land; others remain aquatic.

Amphibians are most noticeable in spring and early summer, when large numbers congregate in the shallows of ponds and lakes to mate and lay eggs. Choruses of frogs set up a terrific din, especially at night or after a rain. Salamanders and newts also search for mates in spring. The eggs are laid in jelly-like strings or masses in the shallows. Young amphibians, particularly tadpoles, feed on algae. Adults eat insects, worms, or other small invertebrates. In turn, they become food for fishes, snakes, birds, and some mammals.

Some of the common amphibians of ponds and lakes are shown on the following pages. For more information about this group, see the Golden Nature Guide *Reptiles and Amphibians*.

SALAMANDERS are tailed amphibians. Some live in the water; others on land, returning to water to lay eggs. The larvae look like diminutive adults. Examples of some of the 85 N.A. species are illustrated.

Hellbender
Cryptobranchus alleganiensis

HELLBENDERS are gilled, aquatic salamanders found mainly in fresh waters of the Ohio Valley. Eat crayfish and other small animals. About 18 inches.

Mudpuppy
Necturus maculosus

MUDPUPPIES, of eastern N.A., reach a length of about 12 inches and retain their gills in adult stage. Feed on fishes, crayfish, insects, and mollusks.

Greater Siren
Siren lacertina

SIRENS are eel-like, heavy-bodied salamanders that lack hind limbs. They have feathery gills. Sirens live in shallow marshes and ponds of the Mississippi Valley and southeastern coast. Grow to 2 feet long. Easily provoked to bite.

RED-SPOTTED NEWT, of eastern N.A., to Great Plains, has a rough skin. Subadult stage, called a "red eft," lives on land. Length 3 to 4 inches.

SPOTTED SALAMANDER lives in soft, moist humus, or leaf litter in central and eastern N.A. Breeds in ponds and lays large masses of eggs. To 7 inches long.

MUD SALAMANDERS burrow in the mud of springs in cool ponds or small streams. Found in central and eastern N.A. Reaches a length of 3 to 5 inches.

RED-BACKED SALAMANDER is common in N.A. (western form sometimes considered a separate species). Found in moist places under rocks, logs, and litter.

TWO-LINED SALAMANDER, found in wet areas in eastern N.A., usually hides during day. Like most newts, feeds on worms, insects, and larvae. About 3 inches.

DUSKY SALAMANDER, from 3 to 5 inches long, is found in the eastern U.S. Its color pattern varies. Dusky Salamander lacks lungs and "breathes" through its skin and mouth tissues. Lives in moist places on land, often in or near water.

Dusky Salamander
Desmognathus fuscus

adult

red eft

Red-spotted Newt *Notophthalmus viridescens*

Spotted Salamander
Ambystoma maculatum

Mud Salamander
Pseudotriton montanus

Two-lined Salamander
Eurycea bislineata

Red-back Salamander
Plethodon cinereus

FROGS AND TOADS are tailless amphibians, with hind legs adapted for hopping (toads) or for jumping (frogs), as well as for swimming. Mating takes place in or near water, where the young develop. The adults of many species also spend much of their life in or near water. The familiar tadpole, lacking limbs or true teeth, is the totally aquatic larval stage. The change from tadpole to adult may require from a few weeks to almost two years depending on species. Here are representatives of the approximately 70 N.A. species.

AMERICAN TOAD is short (2 to 4 inches), squat, and more terrestrial than aquatic. It lives in central and eastern N.A. Breeds in spring and early summer, laying long strings of eggs in water. Western Toad more warty. Pupil of eye horizontal.

FOWLER'S TOAD, found from Massachusetts to Iowa and southward, is 2 to 3 inches long. Like all toads, its skin is dry and warty, but it does not cause warts. Common in sandy areas around ponds. Woodhouse Toad in West is almost identical.

SPADEFOOT TOADS (several species) are found across central N.A. Usually no more than 3.5 inches long, these toads live considerable distances from water but always move to ponds or pools to mate and lay eggs. Pupil of eye vertical.

American Toad
Bufo americanus

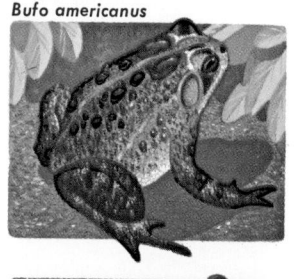

Fowler's Toad
Bufo fowleri

Eastern Spadefoot Toad
Scaphiopus holbrooki

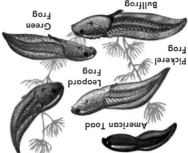

Bullfrog

Green Frog

Pickerel Frog

Leopard Frog

American Toad

TADPOLES

LEOPARD FROG lives in ponds and wet areas but often strays far from water in summer. Probably the most common frog in N.A. Dark spots rimmed with white.

Leopard Frog
Rana pipiens

Pickerel Frog
Rana palustris

Green Frog
Rana clamitans

Bullfrog
Rana catesbeiana

PICKEREL FROG, an eastern species, has rectangular spots and a reddish cast to legs and along sides. About 3 inches long. Red-legged frog, slightly larger, lives on West Coast.

GREEN FROG males have conspicuous eardrums—about the size of the eye. Like other frogs, feeds on insects, worms, and other small animals. Originally found only in central and eastern N.A., but introduced to western states. Length to 3 inches.

BULLFROG, largest frog in N.A., grows to a length of 8 inches. Eardrum (tympanum) as large as or larger than eye. Call is a deep "jug-a-rum." Found in weedy areas along ponds and lakes. Breeds from May to July in North, earlier in the South. Tadpoles take 2 years to mature.

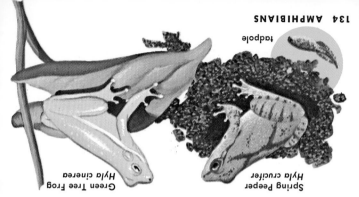

Spring Peeper
Hyla crucifer

Green Tree Frog
Hyla cinerea

tadpole

PACIFIC TREE FROG, no more than 2 inches long, is usually found near bodies of water. Though a tree frog, it is more common on the ground than in trees. Ranges throughout western N.A. and breeds from January to mid-May.

SPRING PEEPER, about 1.5 inches long, is a well-known tree frog. In early spring nearly every eastern woodland pond teems with Spring Peepers, and resounds with the loud, shrill mating calls of the males. Seldom seen except in breeding season.

COMMON TREE FROG, about 2.5 inches long, inhabits all of eastern N.A. except peninsular Florida. Common along shores of streams and ponds, especially in wooded areas. Lays eggs on the surface of quiet, shallow waters of ponds and lakes.

GREEN TREE FROG, about 2 inches long, has a bell-like call. Commonly found on the leaves or stems of plants in or near ponds, lakes, and streams throughout southeastern N.A. Green Tree Frog varies from bright green to nearly yellow.

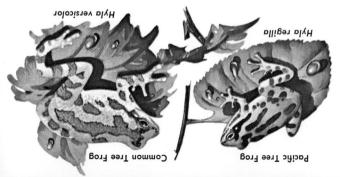

Pacific Tree Frog
Hyla regilla

Common Tree Frog
Hyla versicolor

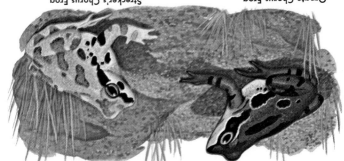

Ornate Chorus Frog
Pseudacris ornata

Strecker's Chorus Frog
Pseudacris streckeri

ORNATE CHORUS FROG, of southeastern U.S., breeds in grassy ditches and along the edges of ponds, usually during late winter. Little is known about the eggs or the tadpoles. The frogs are seldom more than 1 inch long.

STRECKER'S CHORUS FROG has a black mask like the Ornate's, but is larger (about 1.5 inches long) and stouter than are most of the chorus frogs. Common near ponds or lakes, in south-central N.A. Breeds in late winter or early spring.

CRICKET FROG, a warty tree frog about 1 inch long, is distributed throughout central and eastern N.A. Varies in color throughout range. Rasping call is common in weedy margins of streams and ponds. Breeds February through October.

SWAMP CHORUS FROG breeds in ponds and ditches in the spring, then moves to higher ground remainder of year. About 1 inch long. It is found through middle N.A. In Southwest this frog lives high in mountains where it is cool.

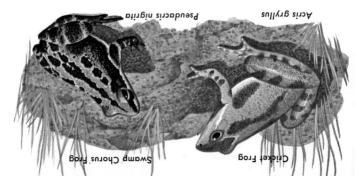

Cricket Frog
Acris gryllus

Swamp Chorus Frog
Pseudacris nigrita

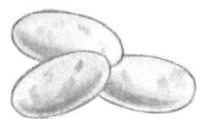

eggs and young
of Pond Slider
(p. 138)

REPTILES are protected by scales or horny plates. Most reptiles lay eggs, covered by a leathery shell. In a few kinds the eggs are kept inside the female's body until hatching. Most reptiles have two pairs of legs, though snakes (and a few lizards) are legless. All except turtles have teeth. Three of the four major groups—turtles, crocodilians, and snakes—are found commonly in ponds and lakes.

In aquatic food pyramids, snakes and some turtles are "top" carnivores, for they feed on other small aquatic animals and are rarely food themselves. Biologists feel that most fishes eaten by reptiles (and also by water birds) are weak or ailing and that this predation does not reduce fish population significantly.

AMERICAN ALLIGATOR inhabits ponds, streams, and wetlands in the Southeast. Alligators 8 to 10 feet long were once common but are rare today. The female builds a large nest of debris close to the water and guards the eggs and young.

American Alligator
Alligator mississippiensis

TURTLES are the most characteristic reptiles of ponds and lakes. Their lower shell, or plastron, is joined to a dome-shaped upper shell, or carapace. Most turtles can draw their head and legs partly or completely inside their shell for protection. Turtles have sharp bony jaws but no teeth. The female digs a hole in dirt or sand, deposits her eggs there, and covers them before she leaves. Eggs are incubated by heat of the sun.

MUSK TURTLES are named for the musky odor the turtles secrete when disturbed. The small plastron is hinged only at the front, and the carapace is usually a dull color. The Stinkpot Musk Turtle occurs from the Atlantic to Wisconsin, south to Gulf. Length, 3 to 4 inches.

Stinkpot Musk Turtle

Stenotherus odoratus

plastron

MUD TURTLES have two hinges to the plastron so that both head and limbs can be pulled inside. They feed on insects and other small animals. Of the five N.A. species, the Eastern Mud Turtle is most common. Length 3 to 4 inches.

Mud Turtle *Kinosternon subrubrum*

plastron

SNAPPING TURTLE may weigh 35 pounds but is usually much smaller. Carapace 10 to 12 inches long. Has a small plastron, a large head, and a long tail. Often buries in the bottom muds; seldom basks. Eats both plants and animals. Widespread in U.S., Alligator Snapper of the South may weigh 150 pounds.

plastron

Snapping Turtle *Chelydra serpentina*

western   eastern

COOTERS AND SLIDERS are basking turtles found throughout central and eastern N.A. They are mainly vegetarians. Older individuals usually have a wrinkled carapace (to 12 inches long), and the rear of the shell is notched. Pond Sliders have a red or yellow spot behind each eye, and the lower jaw is flat on the underside. Cooters have either narrow lengthwise stripes or a series of spots on the head. The lower jaw is rounded. Red-bellied Turtles have red or orange on the plastron and only a few lines on head.

PAINTED TURTLES, found in shallow, weedy waters throughout the U.S. and southern Canada, have a smooth, flattened carapace. The single species in the U.S. is widely distributed and differs in the color and markings on the plastron and carapace in the various parts of its range. Its food is dominantly plant material, but it also eats small animals, either dead or alive. Length 5 to 6 inches.

Painted Turtle
Chrysemys picta

Red-bellied Turtle
Pseudemys rubriventris

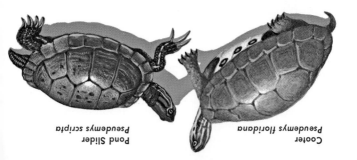

Pond Slider
Pseudemys scripta

Cooter
Pseudemys floridana

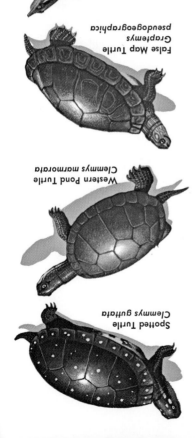

Spotted Turtle
Clemmys guttata

Western Pond Turtle
Clemmys marmorata

False Map Turtle
*Graptemys
pseudogeographica*

Spiny Softshell
Turtle
Trionyx ferox

SPOTTED TURTLE occurs in ponds, marshes, and ditches in central N.A. When not basking, it usually noses lazily among plants or wanders on shore. Feeds mainly on insects but also eats other small animals. The newly hatched have a single yellow spot on each carapace plate; adults have more than one spot. Length 3 to 5 inches.

WESTERN POND TURTLE, which reaches a length of about 6 inches, occurs from British Columbia to Baja California. Its carapace is dark with yellow spots; the plastron is yellowish. Feeds on small animals and on some plants.

MAP TURTLES, or Sawbacks (9 species), are found in central and eastern N.A. These are shy, basking turtles, some with beautiful and ornate markings. Their favorite foods are mussels and snails, which they crush in their broad jaws. They feed to a lesser degree on crustaceans and on other small animals that live in ponds and lakes. Length of carapace 9 to 10 inches.

SOFTSHELL TURTLES are very flat. The upper shell is covered with soft, leathery skin, leaving a wide, soft edge. Two species are widespread in N.A. east of Rockies. More common in streams than in ponds and lakes. Softshells have a long, snakelike neck and can bite viciously. Spiny Softshell Turtle has bumps along front edge of carapace. Length 12 inches or more.

SNAKES live under rocks or debris along the shore; others spend much of their time in the water. Snakes feed mainly on frogs, tadpoles, fishes, crayfish, worms, and insects. Some snakes lay tough-shelled eggs in decaying vegetation or loose soil along the shore. Others, including the common water snakes and garter-snakes, give birth to their young.

Most of the snakes found near water are harmless,

COMMON WATER SNAKE is a heavy-bodied, harmless, but quick-tempered snake of central and eastern N.A. Basks on branches or rocks. Color varies. Length to about 3 feet.

QUEEN SNAKE, a slender water snake, is found in mid-central N.A. Food consists mainly of crayfish. Does not bask as commonly as other water snakes. To about 3 feet in length.

GREEN WATER SNAKE lives in quiet waters and marshes from South Carolina to Texas and Indiana. Like other water snakes, it gives birth to its young. Length to about 3.5 feet.

DIAMOND-BACKED WATER SNAKE is most abundant in Mississippi Valley. It reaches a length of 4 feet but is usually smaller. Looks like Cottonmouth (p. 142) but is more active.

Common Water Snake
Natrix sipedon

Queen Snake
Natrix septemvittata

Green Water Snake
Natrix cyclopion

Natrix rhombifera

Diamond-backed Water Snake

though some are easily provoked to bite. In N.A. the only truly aquatic venomous snake is the Cottonmouth (p. 142), but the Copperhead and several kinds of rattlesnakes sometimes search for food along shores. All of these are pit vipers, identified by the deep pore on each side of the head between the eye and nostril. Vipers also have narrow, vertical pupils. They have a triangular head, but so do some harmless snakes.

BLACK SWAMP SNAKE, found from South Carolina through Florida, reaches a length of about 1 foot. It lives along the shore and feeds on worms, frogs, and other small animals.

STRIPED SWAMP SNAKE is slightly longer (to 1.5 feet) than the Black Swamp Snake. It is found in the same area and is similar in habits. Body stouter; belly yellow.

RAINBOW SNAKE is a heavy-bodied, striped, marsh snake found from Maryland southward. Stripes may be orange to red; tail sharp and horny. A secretive burrower. To about 3.5 feet.

MUD SNAKE is found along the Atlantic and Gulf coasts and up the Mississippi Valley. Back shiny black; spots on belly red. Tail ends in a sharp spine. Burrows in mud. Length, 4 feet.

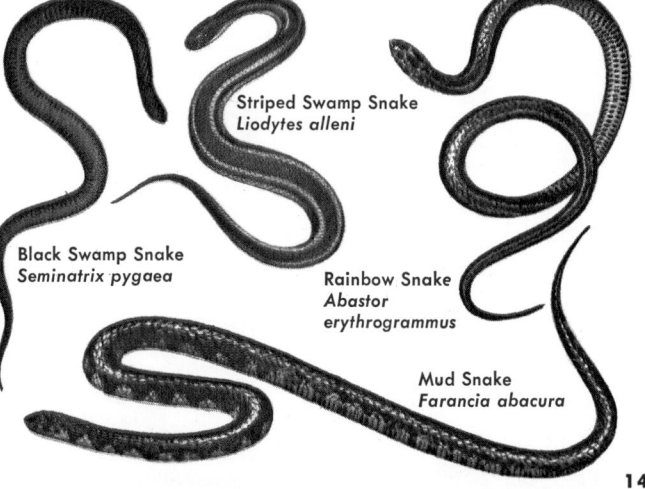

Striped Swamp Snake
Liodytes alleni

Black Swamp Snake
Seminatrix pygaea

Rainbow Snake
Abastor erythrogrammus

Mud Snake
Farancia abacura

Cottonmouth
Ancistrodon
piscivorus

Pygmy Rattlesnake
Sistrurus miliarius

COTTONMOUTH, or Water Moccasin, is found throughout the South. A sluggish, thick-bodied, poisonous snake, averaging 3 feet in length, it feeds on a variety of small aquatic animals, including fishes. When disturbed, it opens mouth and displays cottony-white interior.

PYGMY RATTLESNAKE (length 1 to 1.5 feet) is a poisonous pit viper of wetlands and pond shores in southern and eastern N.A. The Canebrake Rattlesnake (to 6 ft.) also inhabits lowlands of the South. The Massasauga, a bog rattler of central N.A., reaches a length of 2.5 feet.

GARTERSNAKES of nearly a dozen species (1.5 to 3 feet) are widespread in eastern and central N.A. Ribbon Snake is slim eastern, semiaquatic species. Gartersnakes are common along shores, especially in dry weather. They eat worms, fishes, tadpoles, and other small animals.

ROUGH GREEN SNAKE, found from southern New Jersey to the Gulf Coast, lives among shore plants but may take to water to escape enemies or to chase prey. The Smooth Green Snake is less common near water. Both feed on insects and spiders. Length 1 to 3.5 feet.

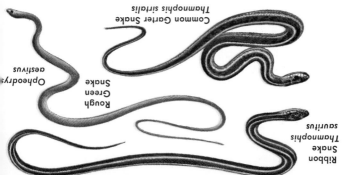

Common Garter Snake
Thamnophis sirtalis

Rough
Green
Snake
Opheodrys
aestivus

Ribbon
Snake
Thamnophis
saurius

BIRDS of a few groups are semiaquatic. They nest along ponds, lakes, or streams and feed on aquatic plants or on fish, crustaceans, and other animals. Most notable are shore birds (herons, sandpipers—pp. 146-150) with long legs for wading, and the waterfowl (swans, geese, ducks—pp. 143-145), with webbed feet for swimming. Waterfowl float high, buoyed up by air trapped in their feathers. Oil, secreted by a special gland and preened into their feathers, may help prevent soaking up water.

Many birds visit ponds and wetlands for food or nest along shore. These include hawks and owls, plus swallows, grackles, thrushes, warblers, and other perching birds. A few of these are shown here. Measurements given with illustrations are length and sometimes wingspread (w). See also the Golden Nature Guides *Birds* and *Gamebirds* and Golden Field Guide *Birds of North America*.

SWANS, the largest waterfowl, are long-necked and commonly feed on plants by "tipping up" in shallows. The Whistling Swan nests in Arctic and winters on central Pacific and Atlantic coasts. The Trumpeter Swan, only other native N.A. species, is an inland bird.

GEESE, some only slightly smaller than swans, are sometimes seen in "V" formations in migration flights. They feed on young plants and on grains in fields nearby. Most common is the Canada Goose. Other less common N.A. geese are Snow, Blue, and White-fronted.

Whistling Swan
Olor columbianus

Canada Goose
Branta canadensis

36 in., w. 85 in.

16-25 in., w. 50-68 in.

Wood Duck
Aix sponsa
13.5 in., w. 28 in.

Pintail
Anas acuta
18.5 in., w. 35 in.

female

male

SURFACE-FEEDING DUCKS have a broad, flat bill. Male and female plumages are distinctly different, but in early summer, males go into a dull plumage replaced in the fall. These ducks take flight directly from the surface, some species leaping several feet into the air. Surface-feeders feed mainly on aquatic plants and may "tip up" in deep water. Includes Gadwall, American Widgeon (Baldplate), Shoveller, and Black Duck.

Wood Ducks usually nest in holes in trees near water. Winter in southern U.S. and in Mexico.

Pintails are speedy, graceful ducks, the males with long, slender tail feathers. Breed in northwestern ponds, winter along both coasts. Occasionally feed on mollusks, insects, crustaceans.

Mallards are seasonally common throughout N.A. The species has many domestic varieties.

Teals are fast fliers and commonly travel in large flocks. The Green-winged prefers fresh water summer and winter. Cinnamon and Blue-winged teals make greater winter use of bays.

Mallard
Anas platyrhynchos

females

male

16 in., w. 36 in.

Green-winged Teal
Anas carolinensis

male

10.5 in., w. 24 in.

DIVING DUCKS feed by diving under the water. The diet of those that frequent ponds consists mainly of wild celery, pondweeds, and other aquatic plants. They also eat more mollusks, crustaceans, and insects than do surface-feeding ducks. Unlike surface-feeders, diving ducks run over surface in taking flight. Ring-necked Duck, Bufflehead and Lesser Scaup are other diving ducks seen around fresh water. Others are marine.

RUDDY DUCK belongs to a distinct group most closely related to tropical masked ducks. It frequents ponds and eats mainly plants, which it gets by diving. Can also sink below surface.

Ruddy Duck
Oxyura jamaicensis
11 in., w. 23 in.

male

female

Common Merganser
Mergus merganser
18 in., w. 37 in.

male

MERGANSERS have a "toothed" bill which they use to catch and hold fish, their principal food. Of the three N.A. species, the Common Merganser prefers fresh water.

The Common Goldeneye nests in holes in trees near water. Eats more animals than plants. Migrates in small high-flying flocks. Canvasbacks fly in a "V" formation, like geese, in long migration flights. Nests in Canada. Head profile flat.

The Redhead breeds from central and western U.S. north into Canada. Female lays 10 to 15 eggs; may also lay eggs in other ducks' nests. Head profile round.

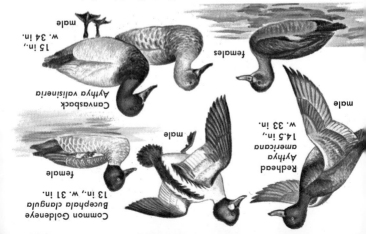

Canvasback
Aythya valisineria
15 in., w. 34 in.

male

females

male

Redhead
Aythya americana
14.5 in., w. 33 in.

male

Common Goldeneye
Bucephala clangula
13 in., w. 31 in.

female

male

WADERS AND OTHER

KING RAIL is a shy marsh bird found from Midwest to the Gulf and eastward. On short flights its feet dangle below; on long flights its legs are tucked under its body. Five other species of rails live in swamps and marshes in N.A. All are elusive and hard to see.

COMMON GALLINULE, a rail-like marsh bird with a short beak, breeds from the Gulf through central and eastern U.S. It swims well or runs over lily pads and feeds on plants. The Purple Gallinule, southern in range, is found on larger lakes and in coastal marshes.

COOT is a ducklike bird found in bays, lakes, and ponds throughout central N.A. It runs over the water before taking flight. Coots swim well and dive for protection. They eat a variety of plants and small animals. White bill is distinctive.

King Rail
Rallus elegans
14 in., w. 24 in.

Common
Gallinule
*Gallinula
chloropus*
12.5 in.,
w. 21 in.

American Coot
Fulica americana
12 in., w. 25 in.

WATER BIRDS

GREAT BLUE HERON introduces a family of long-legged waders with sharp bills for feeding on aquatic animals. Note its large size, colors, and markings. Herons frequent lakes, ponds, and marshes, feeding mainly on fishes and frogs. Thirteen species are found in N.A.

COMMON EGRET breeds from California to Tennessee and southward, wandering into Canada in summer. Note yellow bill, black feet and legs. The smaller (20 in.) Snowy Egret has a black bill and legs, yellow feet. The Cattle Egret (17 in.) still smaller prefers pastures to wetlands.

GREEN HERON is found widely in eastern U.S. and also along the West Coast. Note the orange legs and contrasting body colors. All other dark herons except the Green and the two below prefer saltwater lagoons and mud flats.

BLACK-CROWNED NIGHT HER-ON and also the Yellow-crowned feed on aquatic insects, fish and amphibians. They sleep by day.

AMERICAN BITTERN, found in wetlands north to central Canada, "freezes" when in danger. Young night herons similar in appearance. Least Bittern is smallest heron.

Great Blue Heron
Ardea herodias
38 in., w. 70 in.

Common Egret
Casmerodius albus
32 in., w. 55 in.

Green Heron
Butorides virescens
14 in., w. 25 in.

Black-crowned Night Heron
Nycticorax nycticorax
23 in., w. 45 in.

American Bittern
Botaurus lentiginosus
20 in., w. 44 in.

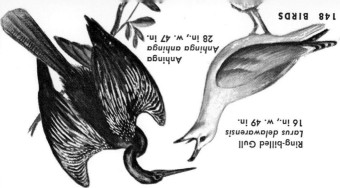

Anhinga
Anhinga anhinga
28 in., W. 47 in.

Ring-billed Gull
Larus delawarensis
16 in., W. 49 in.

SANDPIPERS of nearly 40 N.A. species are birds mostly of ocean shores, but a number of species are found along lakes, ponds, and rivers. All have long slender bills and mottled plumages. Yellowlegs (2 species from tundra southward) have bright yellow legs. Solitary Sandpiper, also widespread, has a dark rump and barred tail feathers. Spotted Sandpiper, more southern, bobs its tail continually. Common Snipe and Woodcock are snipes of bogs, marshes and along shores.

RING-BILLED, Franklin's and several other species of gulls feed and nest on inland ponds and lakes. They may winter along coasts. Plumages of gulls vary with the season and also with the bird's age. Feed on fish and insects or as scavengers.

ANHINGA, or Water Turkey, is found in southeastern U.S. It is commonly seen perched on limbs with its wings spread wide for drying. When swimming, only its slim snakelike neck may be above the water. Spears fish with its long sharp bill.

Greater Yellowlegs
Totanus melanoleucus
11 in.

Solitary Sandpiper
Tringa solitaria
7 in.

COMMON LOONS winter on salt water along both coasts of N.A., also on Great Lakes. Spend summer on inland waters and marshes from Arctic southward to central N.A. Feed mainly on fishes. Call is loud and weird. Of three other species, only Red-throated is likely to be seen. Loons are good swimmers, deep divers.

Common Loon
Gavia immer
24 in., w. 58 in.

PIED-BILLED GREBE has lobed toes and legs set far back (an aid in swimming). Dives quickly. Eats small aquatic animals. Breeds in northern U.S. and Canada, winters in southern U.S. Five other species may be seen along lakes and ponds.

Pied-billed Grebe
Podilymbus podiceps
9 in.

WHITE PELICAN lives on ponds and lakes in western U.S. Major food is fish. Usually nests in colonies, building nests on ground. Brown Pelican is marine.

White Pelican
Pelecanus erythrorhynchos
50 in., w. 110 in.

Common Snipe
Capella gallinago
9 in.

Spotted Sandpiper
Actitis macularia
6.3 in.

Killdeer
Charadrius vociferus
8 in.

Belted Kingfisher
Megaceryle alcyon
12 in.

BELTED KINGFISHER, a large-headed bird with a big beak and loud rattling call, hovers over water and plunges in to catch fish. Widely distributed.

KILLDEER is a plover. Widely distributed in N.A., it lives in open fields and meadows and is commonly seen along the shores of lakes and ponds.

HAWKS AND THEIR KIN have hooked bills and strong talons. The Osprey, widespread in N.A., has conspicuous bend in wings in flight. Dives for fish. Marsh Hawk, with narrow wings, hunts and nests in open marshes.

Swallow-tailed Kite is the most common wetland species. Rare but occurring along waterways is the Bald Eagle, national emblem of U.S.; its food is largely fish. Short-tailed Hawk also resides in wetlands.

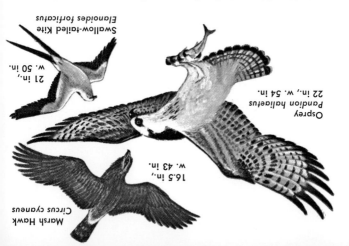

Swallow-tailed Kite
Elanoides forficatus
21 in., w. 50 in.

Osprey
Pandion haliaetus
22 in., w. 54 in.

16.5 in., w. 43 in.

Marsh Hawk
Circus cyaneus

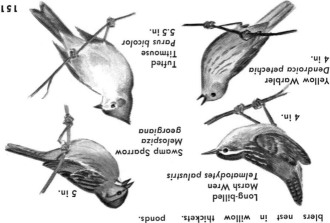

Tufted Titmouse
Parus bicolor
5.5 in.

Yellow Warbler
Dendroica petechia
4 in.

Swamp Sparrow
*Melospiza
georgiana*
5 in.

4 in.

Long-billed
Marsh Wren
Telmatodytes palustris
4 in.

PERCHING BIRDS form the largest group of birds, including 27 families of songbirds in N.A. Many species come to ponds, lakes and waterways to drink. Insect eaters find the hunting good in wetlands. Some warblers nest in willow thickets.

Blackbirds and grackles nest in cattails and rushes. Swallows are commonly seen skimming ponds for insects. Kingbirds and phoebes dart out after insects. Marsh wrens, titmice, and scores of other species are common along ponds.

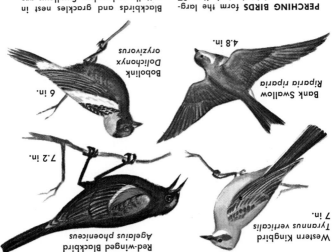

Bobolink
*Dolichonyx
oryzivorus*
6 in.

Bank Swallow
Riparia riparia
4.8 in.

Red-winged Blackbird
Agelaius phoeniceus
7.2 in.

Western Kingbird
Tyrannus verticalis
7 in.

MAMMALS are hairy animals that feed their young on milk from mammary glands. Some feed on plants that grow in the water or along the shore. Others are flesh eaters, preying on fishes, frogs, and other animals. Mammals that live along ponds, lakes, and waterways or in wetlands range in size from tiny shrews to the Moose, largest of the deer. For more about mammals, see the Golden Nature Guide Mammals.

RACCOONS, easily identified by their black mask and tail ringed with black, range throughout middle N.A. They are active at night, frequenting pond and lake shores to feed on frogs, crayfish, and other small animals. Raccoons reach a length of about 30 inches.

Raccoon
*Procyon
lotor*

MINK, large members of the weasel family, feed on crayfish, fishes, young birds, or any other animals they can catch. They travel and hunt alone. Excellent swimmers, mink often go underneath the ice to feed. Found in all moist areas of N.A. About 20 inches long.

RIVER OTTERS are good swimmers, and they often make slides in mud on banks, using them for play or for quick entry into the water. They are widely distributed in N.A. but have become rare in many areas where they were once common. Length to about 3 feet.

River Otter
*Lutra
canadensis*

Mink
Mustela vison

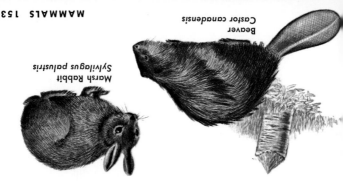

Beaver
Castor canadensis

Marsh Rabbit
Sylvilagus palustris

BEAVERS, with webbed hind feet, are the best-known mammals of fresh water. Feed on the bark and twigs of poplars, birches, and willows. Store winter food in ponds created by their dams. Length 3-4 feet; may weigh 35 pounds. Once found over most of N.A.

MUSKRATS live in lakes, streams, and marshes throughout most of N.A. Good swimmers, they feed on aquatic plants. They either live in burrows dug in a bank or build above-water houses of plant stems. About 2 feet long; reach a weight of about 3 pounds. Trapped for their fur.

SWAMP RABBITS are found from Texas to Illinois and eastward. On southeastern coast, they are replaced by Marsh Rabbit. Both live in woods or grasslands near ponds and in swamps. Feed on plants, bark, and leaves. Both 12 to 15 inches long; their fur is dark, tail grayish.

NUTRIA, a rodent native to S.A., escaped from captivity and is now well established in marshes of southern N.A. Scattered populations are found in Midwest and West. It feeds on vegetation in or near water and has become a pest in some areas. Body length about 2 feet.

Muskrat
Ondatra zibethica

Nutria
Myocastor coypus

LITTLE BROWN BAT, one of more than a dozen species widespread in N.A., comes out at dusk and hunts insects over water and along shores. In winter either hibernates or migrates south. About 3.5 inches long.

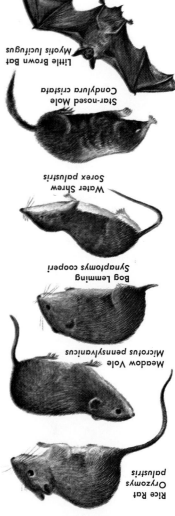

Little Brown Bat
Myotis lucifugus

Star-nosed Mole
Condylura cristata

STAR-NOSED MOLE lives in wet meadows and marshes throughout eastern N.A. Eats insects and worms; travels along surface runways and also in underground burrows. Length to 5 inches.

WATER SHREW, an excellent swimmer, preys on small aquatic animals. Nocturnal, it has tiny eyes and ears, like other shrews. Found in Canada and northern U.S., southward in mountains. Length, 3-4 inches.

Water Shrew
Sorex palustris

SOUTHERN BOG LEMMING, or Bog Vole, lives in wet meadows, swamps, and bogs throughout central and eastern N.A. except in the Deep South. About 4 inches long.

Bog Lemming
Synaptomys cooperi

MEADOW VOLE, also called Meadow or Field Mouse, occurs widely in the cooler parts of N.A., favoring moist meadows. Eats seeds and tender plants. About 5 inches long.

Meadow Vole
Microtus pennsylvanicus

RICE RAT, an excellent swimmer, lives in wet meadows from the Mississippi Valley eastward to New York. Feeds mainly on green plants. Builds a nest of plant stems in stumps or in shallow burrows above the water level. Length 9 to 11 inches.

Rice Rat
Oryzomys palustris

For precise identification of the many kinds of plants and animals found in and near ponds and lakes, these comprehensive, more technical reference books will be helpful. Also see bibliographies in other Golden Guides.

Blair, W. F., Blair, N. P., Brodkorb, P., Cagle, F. R. and Moore, G. A., *Vertebrates of the United States*, McGraw-Hill Book Company, New York, 1957

Coker, R. E., *Streams, Lakes, Ponds*, Univ. N. C. Press, Chapel Hill, 1954

Edmondson, W. T. (Ed.), *Fresh-Water Biology*, John Wiley, New York, 1959

Fasset, N. C., *A Manual of Aquatic Plants*, Univ. Wisc. Press, Madison, Wisc., 1957

Klots, Elsie B., *The New Field Book of Freshwater Life*, G. P. Putnam, New York, 1966

Macan, T. T., and Worthington, E. B., *Life in Lakes and Rivers*, Collins, London, 1951

Muenscher, W. C., *Aquatic Plants of the United States*, Comstock, Ithaca, N. Y., 1944

Needham, P. G. and Needham, P. R., *A Guide to the Study of Freshwater Biology*, Holden-Day, San Francisco, 1962

Odum, E. P., *Fundamentals of Ecology*, W. B. Saunders, Philadelphia, 1971

Pennak, R. W., *Fresh-Water Invertebrates of the United States*, 2nd Ed., Ronald Press, New York, 1978

Reid, G. K., and Wood, R. D., *Ecology of Inland Waters and Estuaries*, Van Nostrand Reinhold, New York, 1967

Smith, G. M., *Freshwater Algae of the United States*, McGraw-Hill, New York, 1950

SCIENTISTS at universities and at state conservation, wildlife, fisheries, and agriculture departments are usually willing to help identify specimens. Always write or call before sending specimens. Specimens usually cannot be returned.

INDEX

The many plants and animals that have no common names are listed in this index by their scientific name (genus). For others, the common name or group name is listed. Scientific names are given also with the illustrations.

Acineta, 76
Adder's tongue, 44
Aeolosoma, 82
Agmenellum, 33
Alderflies, 94, 100, 101
Alders, 69
Algae, 31-37
Alligator, 136
    gar, 128
    weed, 62
Amoeba, 74, 76
Amphibians, 120,
    129-135
Amphibious smartweed,
    59
Amphipods, 86, 91
Anabaena, 32
Anacystis, 32
Anax, 94, 98
Anhinga, 148
Animals, 74-154
Ankistrodesmus, 35
Annelids, 75, 82
Anostraca, 86, 88
Apple snail, 115
Arborvitae, 71
Arcella, 74
Argulus, 90
Arrow arum, 56
Arrowheads, 51
Arthropods, 75, 85-113
Arums, 56
Asellus, 91
Ashes, 70
Aspens, 68
Asplanchna, 80
Asterionella, 37

Backswimmers, 104
Bacteria, 38
Bald cypress, 69
    eagle, 150
Balpate, 144
Balsam cottonwood, 68
Banded killifish, 126
Bank swallow, 151
Bass, 19, 125
Bat, 154
Beak rushes, 54
Beaver, 153
Beetles, 95, 105-106

Bellflower, 66
Belted kingfisher, 150
    skimmers, 98
Berchtold's pondweed,
    48, 49
Bigmouth buffalo, 122
Birches, 70
Birds, 120, 143-151
Bittern, 147
Black ash, 70
    bullhead, 127
    crappie, 125
    -crowned night
    heron, 147
    duck, 144
    flies, 111
    gum, 69
    swamp snake, 141
    willow, 68
Blackroot rush, 55
Bladderworts, 64
Blasturus, 97
Blue beech, 70
    flag, 64
    goose, 143
    green algae, 31,
    32, 33
Bluegill, 124
Bluejoint grass, 53
Bluet, 99
Blue-winged teal, 144
Boat-leaved sphagnum,
    40
Bobolink, 151
Bog lemming, 154
    mosquito, 109
    rosemary, 72, 73
    vole, 154
Bony fishes, 121-128
Bosmina, 89
Bowfin, 128
Brachionus, 80
Brine shrimp, 88
Broad-leaved cattail, 46
Broad-shouldered water
    striders, 102
Brook lamprey, 120
    trout, 124
Brown bullhead, 127
    fingernail clam, 117
    hydra, 78

Bryophytes, 30, 39
Bryozoans, 75, 81
Buffalo, 122
Buffalo gnats, 111
Bufflehead, 145
Bugs, 95, 102-104
Bullfrog, 133
Bullheads, 127
Bur-reeds, 47
Bushy pondweed, 50
Buttonbush, 72, 73

Cabbage palmetto, 71
Caddisflies, 95, 107
Canada goose, 143
Canary grass, 53
Canvasbacks, 145
Carbon dioxide, 12, 13
Carex, 54
Carp, 123
Catenulas, 84
Catfish, 20, 127
Cattails, 21, 46
Cattle egret, 147
Cedars, 71
Ceratium, 31, 36
Chaetogasters, 82
Chair-makers' rush, 54
Channel catfish, 127
Chaoborus, 108
Chara, 36
Chimney crayfish, 93
Chlorella, 34
Chubsuckers, 122
Chydorus, 88, 89
Ciliata, 74, 76
Cinnamon fern, 45
    teal, 144
Cladocera, 86, 88
Cladophora, 34
Clams, 75, 116-117
Clam shrimps, 86, 88, 89
Cloeon, 97
Closterium, 35
Coelenterates, 75, 78, 79
Coleoptera, 95, 105-106
Collecting equipment,
    27, 28, 29
Collembola, 95, 100, 101
Common Water Snake,
    140

Conchostraca, 86, 88
Coontail, 63
Coot, 146
Cooters, 138
Copepods, 86, 90
Copperhead, 140
Cord grass, 52
Corydalus, 94
Cottonmouth, 140, 141, 142
Cottonwood, 68
Cow lily, 60
Crane flies, 110
Crappies, 125
Crawling water beetles, 105
Crayfish, 75, 85, 86, 92–93
Creek chub, 123
Creeping water bugs, 104
Crested woodfern, 44
Cricket frog, 135
Crisp pondweed, 48, 49
Crocodilians, 136
Crustaceans, 85, 86–93
Cut grass, 52
Cyclops, 90
Cymbella, 37
Cypress, 69
Cypridopsis, 87
Cyprinotus, 87

Dace, 123
Damselflies, 94, 98, 99
Daphnia, 89
Darters, 125
Decapoda, 86, 92
Deer fly, 112
Dero, 82
Desmids, 35
Devil's darning needles, 98
Diamond-backed water snake, 141
Diaptomus, 90
Diatoms, 31, 37
Dichelyma, 41
Difflugia, 76
Dinoflagellates, 31, 36
Diptera, 95, 108–112
Dixa midges, 111
Dobsons, 100, 101
Dogfish, 128
Dogwood, 72
Dragonflies, 94, 98, 99
Draparnaldia, 34
Drone fly, 112
Dryopids, 106
Duck potato, 51
Ducks, 144–145
Duckweeds, 17, 57

Dugesias, 84
Dulichium, 54
Dusky salamander, 131

Eared pond snail, 115
Earthworms, 75. 82
Eastern cottonwood, 68
    crayfish, 93
    larch, 71
Eel, 126
Egret, 147
Elmids, 106
Elodea, 55
Enallagma, 99
Ephemera, 97
Ephemerella, 93, 97
Ephemeroptera, 94, 96
Erpobdella, 83
Eryngo, 64
Eubranchipus, 89
Eucypris, 87
Euglena, 31, 36, 74
Euglenoids, 31, 36

Fairy shrimps, 86, 88, 89
False loosestrife, 67
    map turtle, 139
Fanwort, 60, 61, 63
Farancia, 141
Farm pond, 9
Ferns, 42–45
Field mouse 154
Fisher spider, 113
Fishes, 75, 121–128
Fishflies, 100, 101
Flagellates, 74
Flatworms, 75, 84
Flies, 95, 108–112
Floating brownleaf, 48, 49
Florida gar, 128
Flosculario, 80
Flukes, 84
Fontinalis, 41
Food webs, 22–23
Forktails, 99
Fountain moss, 41
Fowler's toad, 132
Fox grape, 73
Fragilaria, 37
Franklin's gull, 148
Fredericella, 81
Frogbit, 59
Frogs, 75, 129, 132–135
Fungi, 38

Gadwall, 144
Gallinule, 146
Gambusia, 126
Gammarus, 91
Gars, 128
Gartersnakes, 142

Gastrotrichs, 119
Geese, 143
Gemmules, 77
Giant bur-reed, 47
    pond snail, 115
    water bugs, 103
Gilled snails, 114, 115
Gizzard shad, 128
Glasswort, 62
Glochidia, 116
Goldeneye, 145
Golden shiner, 123
Goldfish, 123
Gomphosphaeria, 33
Gordian worms, 119
Grape, 73
Grasses, 52, 53
Grassy arrowhead, 51
Great blue heron, 147
    duckweed, 57
Greater siren, 130
    yellowlegs, 148
Green algae, 31, 34, 35
    darner, 98
    frog, 133
    heron, 147
    hydra, 79
    jacket, 98
    snakes, 142
    sunfish, 124
    tree frog, 134
    water snake, 140
    -winged teal, 144
Greenbrier, 73
Gulls, 148

Habitats, 17–21
    bottom, 19
    littoral, 20
    open water, 18
    surface, 17
Haemopsis, 83
Hairy water beetle, 106
    wheel snail, 115
Hawks, 150
Hellbender, 130
Hellgrammites, 94, 100
Helobdella, 83
Hemiptera, 95, 102–104
Herons, 147
Hexagenias, 93, 96
Hirudineas, 83
Honeysuckle, 73
Hornbeam, 70
Horned pondweed, 48, 49
Hornworts, 63
Horse fly, 112
Horsehair worms, 119
Horsetails, 43
House mosquito, 109
Hyalella, 91

Hydrachna, 113
Hydras, 75, 78, 79
Hydrodictyon, 35
Hydrogen, 10
Hygrobates, 112
Hygrohypnum, 41
Hyssop, 67

Insects, 75, 85, 94–112
Irises, 64
Isonychia, 97
Isopods, 86, 91
Ivy duckweed, 57

Jellyfishes, 78, 79
Johnny darter, 125
Joint-legged animals, 85–113
Jungermannia, 39

Keratella, 80
Killdeers, 150
Killifish, 126
Kingbird, 151
Kingfisher, 150
King rail, 146
Knobbed lampshell, 117

Lake, 4–29
  chubsucker, 122
  sturgeon, 128
  trout, 120
Lampreys, 120
Lampshells, 117
Larch, 71
Largemouth bass, 19, 125
Leaf beetles, 106
Leafy pondweed, 48, 49
Leather jackets, 110
Leatherleaf, 72
Leeches, 75, 82, 83
Lemming, 154
Leopard frog, 129, 133
Lepidoptera, 95, 112
Leptocella, 107
Leptodora, 89
Leptothrix, 38
Lesser duckweed, 57
  scaup, 145
Limber honeysuckle, 73
Limnephilus, 107
Limnochares, 113
Limnology, 5
Limpets, 115
Liodytes, 141
Little brown bat, 154
  pond snail, 115
  water lily, 60, 61
Liverworts, 39
Lizards, 136

Long-billed marsh wren, 151
Longnose gar, 128
Loon, 149
Loosestrife, 64
Lotus, 60, 61
Lyngbya, 33

Macrobdella, 83
Mad-dog skullcap, 66
Madtom, 127
Malaria mosquito, 109
Mallards, 144
Mammals, 120, 152–154
Manna grass, 52
Maples, 70
Map turtle, 139
Marchantia, 39
Mare's tail, 65
Marsh cinquefoil, 66
  fern, 44
  hawk, 150
  rabbit, 153
  St. John's-wort, 66
  treaders, 102
  wren, 151
Massasauga, 142
Mastigophora, 76
Mayflies, 85, 94, 96, 97
Meadow mouse, 154
  vole, 154
Megaloptera, 94, 100
Merganser, 145
Meridion, 37
Mermaid weed, 64
Meyenia, 74, 77
Micrasterias, 35
Midges, 111
Minerals, 14
Mink, 152
Minnows, 123
Mites, 85, 113
Mitrula, 38
Molanna, 107
Mole, 154
Mollusks, 75, 114–117
Monostyla, 80
Moonwort, 44
Moraria, 90
Mosquitoes, 17, 108–109
Mosquitofish, 126
Mosquito hawks, 98
Moss animals, 75, 81
Mosses, 40, 41
Moths, 95, 112
Mougeotia, 34
Mud plantain, 58
  salamander, 131
  snake, 141
  turtle, 137
Mudpuppy, 130

Muskellunge, 126
Muskrat, 153
Musk turtle, 137

Naiads, 19, 50
Narrow-leaved cattail, 46
Nauplius, 87
Navicula, 31, 37
Nemas, 118
Nematocysts, 78, 79
Nematodes, 118
Nemerteans, 118
Neureclipsis, 107
Neuroptera, 94, 100
Newts, 129, 131
Nitella, 31, 36
Northern pike, 18, 126
No-see-ums, 111
Nostoc, 32
Notostraca, 86, 88
Nutria, 153
Nymphula, 112

Oaks, 69
Ochterids, 104
Odonata, 94, 98, 99
Oecetis, 107
Oligochaetes, 82
One-celled animals, 74, 76
Orange-spotted sunfish, 124
Orb snail, 115
Ornate chorus frog, 13.
Oscillatoria, 31, 33
Osprey, 150
Ostracods, 86, 87
Ostrich fern, 45
Otter, 152
Overcup oak, 69
Oxygen, 10, 12, 13

Pacific tree frog, 134
Painted turtle, 138
Papershells, 117
Paramecium, 74, 76
Pearly mussels, 117
Peat mosses, 40
Pectinatella, 81
Pediastrum, 35
Pelicans, 149
Pelocoris, 104
Perching birds, 151
Peridinium, 36, 76
Perla, 94
pH, 13
Phacus, 36
Phantom crane flies, 1
  gnats, 108, 109
Philodina, 80

Philonotis, 41
Photosynthesis, 12, 22, 30
Phytoplankton, 18, 22
Pickerel frog, 133
Pickerels, 126
Pickerelweeds, 21, 58
Pied-billed grebe, 149
Pike, 18, 126
Pill clam, 117
Pines, 71
Pintail, 144
Pitcher plant, 65
Planaria, 75
Plankton, 18, 19, 22
Plants, 30–73
  zones, 20, 21
Plecoptera, 94, 100, 101
Plumatella, 81
Podophyra, 76
Podura, 101
Pointed winkle, 115
Poison ivy, 72
  sumac, 72, 73
Polyarthra, 80
Pond, 4–29
  crayfish, 92
  skaters, 102
  sliders, 136, 138
Pondweeds, 20, 48, 49
Poplars, 68
Porifera, 77
Poteriodendron, 76
Prawns, 93
Predaceous diving
  beetles, 105
Primrose willow, 66
Proboscis worms, 118
Procotyla, 84
Prosobranchs, 115
Protozoa, 74, 76
Ptychoptera, 111
Pulmonate snails,
  114, 115
Pumpkinseed sunfish,
  124
Punkies, 111
Purple gallinule, 146
Pygmy backswimmers,
  104
  rattlesnake, 142
Queen snake, 140
Quillworts, 43
Rabbit, 153
Raccoons, 152
Rails, 146
Rainbow snake, 141
  trout, 141
Rat, 154

Rat-tailed maggot, 112
Rattlesnake, 140, 142
  fern, 44
Red alder, 70
  -bellied turtle, 138
  birch, 70
  eft, 131
  dogwood, 72
  maple, 70
  legged frog, 133
  -spotted newt, 131
  -throated loon, 149
  -winged blackbird,
  151
Redfin pickerel, 126
Redbelly dace, 123
  shiner, 123
Redhead, 145
Redhorse, 122
Reed grass, 53
Reptiles, 120, 136–142
Respiration, 12
Rhyacophila, 107
Ribbon snake, 142
  worms, 118
Riccia, 39
Ricciocarpus, 39
Rice rat, 154
Ring-billed gull, 148
Ring-necked duck, 145
River birch, 41
  otters, 152
  snail, 115
Rivularia, 33
Rotifers, 33, 80
Rough green snake, 142
Roundworms, 118
Royal fern, 45
Ruddy duck, 145
Rushes, 55
Sabal palmetto, 71
Sago pondweed, 48, 49
Salamanders, 129,
  130–131
Sialidids, 104
Salt-marsh mosquito,
  109
Salvinia, 43
Sandpipers, 148
Saprolegnia, 38
Sarcodina, 74, 76
Sawbacks, 139
Saw grass, 55
Scapholeberis, 89
Scenedesmus, 35
Scented pond lily, 60,
  61
Scouring rush, 43
Scuds, 86, 91
Sea lamprey, 120

Sedges, 21, 54, 55
Seed shrimp, 86, 87
Segmented worms, 75,
  82, 83
  86, 87
Sharp-fruited rush 55
Sharp-leaved
  sphagnum, 40
Shiners, 19, 123
Shore bugs, 104
Short-awn foxtail, 52
Shortnose gar, 128
Short-tailed hawk, 150
Shoveller, 144
Shrew, 154
Shrimps, 85, 86, 92, 93
Shrubs, 72, 73
Side-swimmers, 91
Simulium, 111
Siren, 130
Sisyra, 94
Skullcaps, 66
Sliders, 138
Small bedstraw, 66
Smallmouth bass, 125
Smartweeds, 59
Sminthurides, 101
Smoky alderfly, 101
Smooth green snake,
  101
  142
Snails, 75, 114–115
Snakes, 75, 140–142
Snapping turtle, 137
Snipe, 148
Snow goose, 143
Snowy egret, 147
Softshell turtle, 139
Soldier flies, 112
Solitary sandpiper, 148
Sour gum, 69
Southern bog lemming,
  154
  naiad, 50
Sow bugs, 86, 91
Spadefoot toad, 132
Speckled alder, 70
Sphaerotilus, 38
Sphagnums, 40
Sphere clams, 117
Spicules, 77
Spiders, 85, 113
Spike rushes, 55
Spinulose woodfern, 44
Spiny naiad, 50
  softshell turtle, 139
Spirogyra, 31, 34
Sponges, 74, 77
Spongilla, 77
  flies, 94, 100, 101
Spotted gar, 128
  salamander, 131
  sandpiper, 148
  turtle, 139

Spring peeper, 134
Springtails, 95, 100, 101
Star-nosed mole, 154
Statoblasts, 81
Stentor, 76
Stilt spider, 113
Stinkpot musk turtle, 137
Stoneflies, 94, 100, 101
Stoneworts, 31, 36
Strecker's chorus frog, 135
Striped swamp snake, 141
Sturgeon, 128
Suckers, 122
Suctoria, 76
Sumacs, 72, 73
Sundew, 65
Sunfish, 21, 124, 125
Swallow-tailed kite, 150
Swampcandle loosestrife, 67
Swamp cottonwood, 68
  crayfish, 92
  cricket frog, 135
  maple, 71
  oak, 69
  pine, 71
  rabbit, 153
  rose, 72, 73
  sparrow, 151
  sumac, 72, 73
Swans, 143
Sweet bay, 73
  flag, 56
  gale, 72
Sycamores, 69

Tabellaria, 37
Tadpole madtom, 127
  shrimp, 86, 88, 89
Tadpoles, 133
Tamarack, 69
Tapeworms, 84
Tardigrades, 119
Tendipes, 111
Thallophytes, 30
Thiothrix, 38
Threadtailed stonefly, 101
Three-square, 54
Tiger beetles, 106
  salamander, 129
Tipula, 110
Toad bugs, 104

Toads, 129, 132
Topminnows, 126
Tracheophytes, 30
Tree frogs, 134
Trees, 68, 69, 70, 71
Triaenodes, 107
Trichoptera, 95, 107
Trout, 121
Trumpeter swan, 143
Tube worm (tubifex), 19, 75, 82
Tufted titmouse, 151
Tumblers, 108
Tupelos, 69
Turbellarians, 84
Turtles, 75, 136, 137–139
Two-lined salamander, 131

Variable pondweed, 48, 49
Vascular plants, 30, 42
Vertebrates, 75, 120–154
Virginia chain fern, 45
Voles, 154
Volvox, 35

Warmouth, 124
Water, 6, 7, 10, 11, 14, 15, 16, 17
  bears 119
  birds, 146–151
  boatmen, 103
  celery, 20
  cress, 62
  density, 10
  fern, 43
  fleas, 86, 88, 89
  hemlock, 64
  hyacinth, 58
  hypnum, 41
  lettuce, 56
  lilies, 20, 60, 61
  lobelia, 65
  marigold, 63, 67
  measurers, 102
  milfoil, 20, 63, 65
  mites, 113
  moccasin, 142
  molds, 38
  moss, 41
  oak, 69
  parsnip, 67
  pennywort, 66
  plantains, 51
  scavenger beetle, 17, 106

Water (cont.)
  scorpions, 17, 103
  shamrock, 42
  shield, 60, 61
  shrew, 154
  smartweed, 59
  snakes, 140
  starwort, 67
  striders, 102
  tigers, 105
  treaders, 103
  tupelo, 69
  turkey, 148
  weeds, 50, 59
  willow, 67
Western birch, 70
  bur-reed, 47
  crayfish, 92
  pond turtle, 139
  water lily, 60, 61
Whirligig beetles, 17, 105
Whistling swan, 143
White cedar, 71
  crappie, 125
  oak, 69
  pelican, 149
  sucker, 122
  water crowfoot, 63
  water lily, 60, 61
Widgeon, 144
Wild celery, 59
  rice, 53
Willow oak, 69
Willows, 68
Wilson's snipe, 149
Winged lampshell, 117
Winkles, 115
Winterberry, 72, 73
Winterhill, 16
Wolffia, 57
Woodcock, 148
Wood duck, 144
Worms, 75, 82, 83, 84, 118, 119
Wrigglers, 108

Yellow bullhead, 127
Yellow-crowned night heron, 147
Yellow fever mosquito, 109
Yellowlegs, 148
Yellow perch, 125
  warbler, 151
  water crowfoot, 63
  water lily, 60, 61

Zooplankton, 18

2J 2K 2L 2M

MEASURING SCALE (IN 10THS OF AN INCH)